HIT ME WITH
YOUR BEST
SHOT!

HIT ME WITH YOUR BEST SHOT !

THE ULTIMATE GUIDE TO KARAOKE DOMINATION

By Raina Lee

CHRONICLE BOOKS

SAN FRANCISCO

Page 159 constitutes a continuation of the copyright page.

Library of Congress Cataloging-in-Publication Data:
Lee, Raina.
  Hit me with your best shot : the ultimate guide to karaoke domination / by Raina Lee.
     p. cm.
  ISBN: 978-0-8118-6140-3
1. Karaoke—Instruction and study. 2. Singing—Instruction and study. 3. Popular music—Instruction and study. I. Title.

  MT820.L46 2008
  783.'043—dc22

                                            2007036030

Manufactured in China
Design and Illustration by Michael Perry.
Cover photograph, back cover photograph, and pages 6, 13, 22, 36–37, 50, 58–59, 76–77, 112, 126, 149, and 153–155 by Sean Lee. Page 74 by Jalo Kotinurmi. Pages 138–139 by Michael Perry.

10 9 8 7 6 5 4 3 2 1

Chronicle Books LLC
680 Second Street
San Francisco, California 94107

www.chroniclebooks.com

THIS BOOK IS
DEDICATED TO MY PARENTS,
MEICHUNG AND YANG HAI LEE,
WHO UNWITTINGLY INSPIRED A
LIFETIME OF OFF-KEY CROONING.

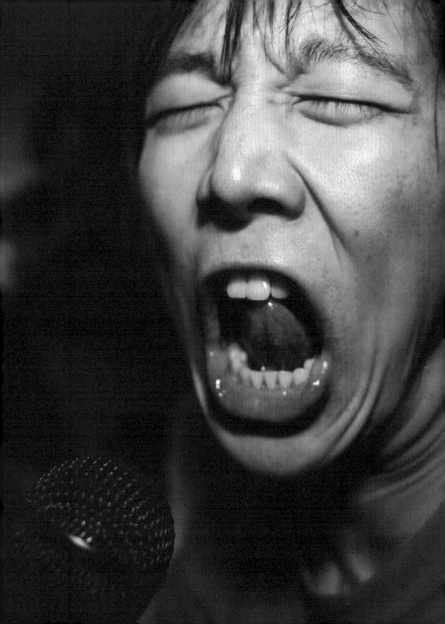

WE'VE ONLY JUST BEGUN

8... FOREWORD

12... CHAPTER 1   GET STARTED

23... CHAPTER 2   THE HISTORY

36... CHAPTER 3   RULE THE SCENE

50... CHAPTER 4   SING LIKE A PRO

58... CHAPTER 5   GET DATES, WIN AFFECTION

76... CHAPTER 6   MAKE A KILLER SET LIST

113... CHAPTER 7   KARAOKE TO GO-GO

127... CHAPTER 8   THROW THE ULTIMATE KARAOKE PARTY

138... RESOURCES : THE LINER NOTES

155... POP QUIZ

158... ACKNOWLEDGMENTS

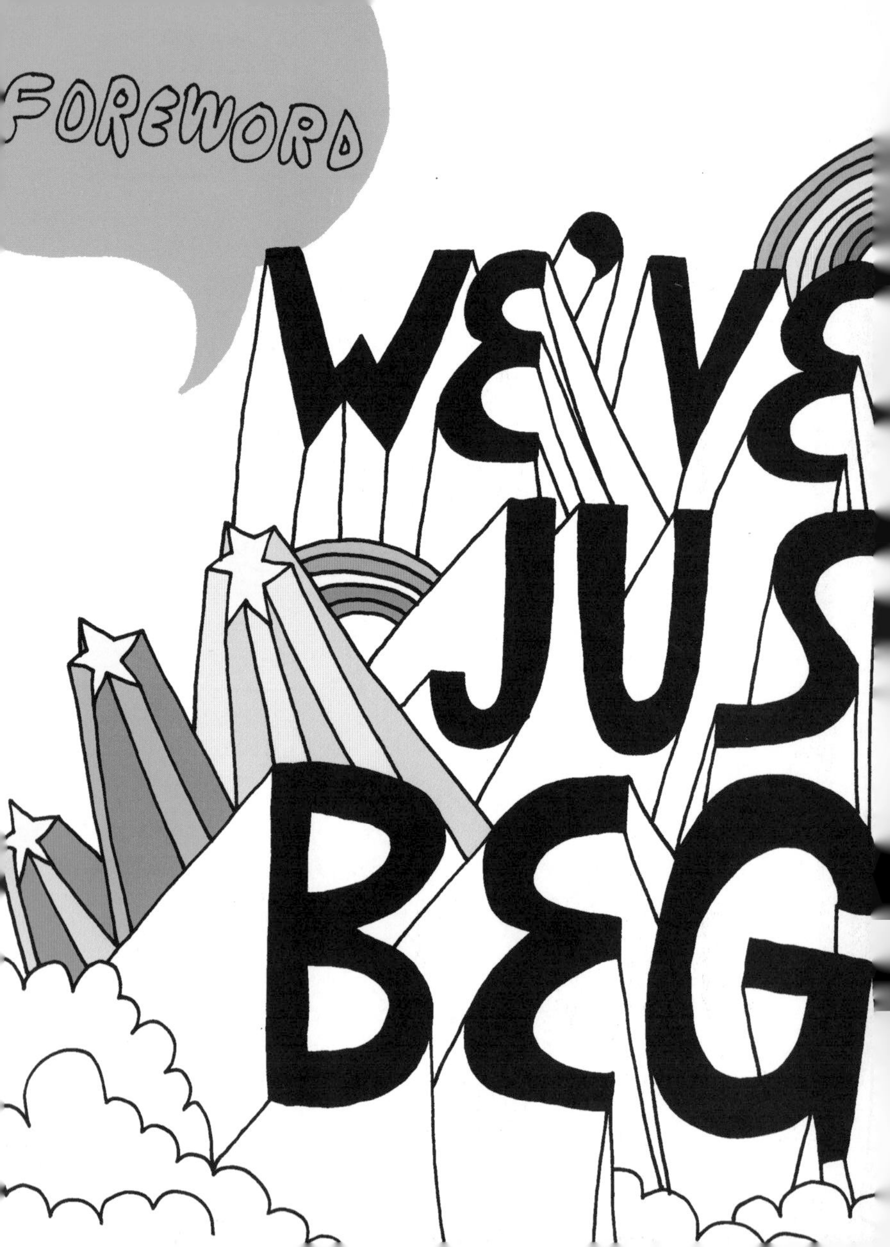
FOREWORD
WE'VE
JUS
BEG

My childhood dentist, Dr. Sun, had a karaoke machine in his waiting room. His makeshift office in Monterey Park (a.k.a. Little Taipei of L.A.) was a hodgepodge assembly of sticky, plastic-covered couches, old magazines, a dusty TV from 1985, and a dream-worthy karaoke machine reserved for "special patients." Because I was a good customer (read: had bad teeth) and Dr. Sun had a crush on my mom, I was an A-lister. In the minutes I had on the machine, cavity-mouthed kids and elderly Chinese waiting for root canals faded into the background. It was showtime and I was the star.

Dr. Sun's collection of laser discs was not what my friends listened to. He had *Old Style Love Songs* showcasing the brilliance of Elvis, the Isley Brothers, Paul Anka, and Dusty Springfield, among others. Though my parents grew up in Taiwan, they loved early-'60s American pop songs. After repeated playings of the *Oldies But Goodies* tapes my dad ordered from TV, they became the songs of my childhood, too.

For years, the pre-novocaine karaoke made my weekly visits less painful. I'd sing "All I Have to Do Is Dream" over drilling sounds from the next room. Singing made me feel at home. . . because that's what we did at home. While other families played board games, my family **karaoked.** We sang after dinner, at dinner, in the afternoon, and in our pajamas. We even took our karaoke machine on vacation, like it was another member of the family. Singing was not a frivolous pastime, but a fundamental part of living. It shouldn't have surprised me that Dr. Sun had a karaoke machine in his waiting room. For many Asian Americans, karaoke is life.

Nine fillings later, I stopped going to Dr. Sun. This is not to say my teeth improved, but my singing was about to. I discovered karaoke bars and **noraebang** (Korean for private karaoke rooms). After college, I was shocked to meet people who had never karaoked. What kind of sad homes did they come from? I realized that karaoke must be a quirky Asian cultural thing. It didn't have to be. From then on, I decided to be the Karaoke Instigator. I became that crazy person who drags people onstage, or makes them take shots if they're too shy to sing in public. I've met many co-conspirators along the way, and I'm still meeting them; the pool of talent only gets deeper and wider. Coworkers, Karaoke Scene message-boarders, musicians, and strangers at bars are all my karaoke people. And if you're reading this, you are too.

I'm most certainly a karaoke advocate. I believe everyone should karaoke. I'm not saying it will solve the world's problems (although, it might; see "Karaoke for World Peace," page 29). It can, however, make your life better, if only for the duration of "Rump Shaker." Karaoke will change your reality one song at a time. I know for certain that it can transform a terrifying wait at the dentist's into a rose-tinted medley of *Old Style Love Songs*.

xoxo, Raina

P.S. I bolded all the essential karaoke vocab words throughout the book. If they're new to you, flip to the Glossary, page 150, to learn more.

CHAPTER 1

GET STARTED

Karaoke is about understanding the delicate balance between singing songs you love and songs that will please the crowd. It's about working the room and establishing social dominance. And most of all, it's about knowing how to have a good time.

To achieve true karaoke awesomeness, you have to grasp the heart of karaoke: the importance of spontaneous singing anywhere, anytime. Think of life as a musical, where people on the street spontaneously break out into song and dance. The main character is you, singing and dancing every minute of your life.

Once you bring the joys of karaoke into your life, it's your duty to, well, sing its praises. Proselytize to those who have never felt the pseudo–rock star high. This is not for any religious cult-y reason. Heavens no. You just don't want to be the only one singing "I Touch Myself" at the top of your lungs. How embarrassing. You'll want some backup singers around to share the blame.

THE SIX POINTS OF KARAOKE

So you want to be a karaoke star. You figure with the prerecorded songs plus some liquid courage, how hard can it be? You just have to stand there, right?

Wrong. Karaoke is easy, but it takes more than just showing up to be *amazing*. It takes know-how. And you probably already know more than you think. Karaoke is just like other forms of singing you do all the time—sing-along *Sound of Music* screenings, your church **a cappella** choir, car-singing during gridlock . . . Well, look at you! You're practically a star already!

To rock yourself into the next singing stratosphere, heed these six karaoke commandments.

1. FAKE IT LIKE YOU KNOW IT.

Karaoke is about spontaneity. It's about never letting your fans see you sweat. When you don't know the words, fake 'em. When you can't follow the melody, hum "Mary Had A Little Lamb." When you trip over the speakers, well, F it. And if spontaneity scares you, embrace the impromptu by performing the same song differently every time.

2. FLAUNT YOUR PERSONAL STYLE.

Karaoke is all about "My Way." That is to say, your way. Every song in the book has been done before, so your performance has to be personal. Do it in a way that's only you. So dance, writhe, do that offensive wiggle your mom told you never to do inside the house.

3. MASTER THE COVER SONG.

Musicians have been covering songs since music began. Covering is a way to pay respect to the songs you love. Karaoke gives this cover power to the musically challenged masses. The songs you sing represent who you are and where you came from. Or if you're a forty-year-old suburban white guy doing "Baby Got Back," it's about faking where you came from.

4. PLAY THE ROLE.

It's boring being you all the time. That's why people love karaoke—it lets them be someone else. It's more glamorous to be Linda Ronstadt circa 1978 in roller skates and hot pants than Jenny the administrative assistant. Suspend your reality, your crappy job, and even your gender, if only for the length of one glorious song.

5. BE DEMOCRATIC.

Cachet counts in Hollywood, but not on Thirsty Thursdays at Jake's Lakehouse in the Poconos. Karaoke is egalitarian. Everyone starts with a clean slate and is judged accordingly.

6. EMBRACE THE BUZZ (IF YOU'RE LEGAL, OF COURSE).

Drinking is not mandatory. But like MSG enhances Chinese food, booze enhances karaoke. The karaoke songs sound just like the original music and you sound just like Olivia Newton-John. The effect: **Beermuffs** (see page 18).

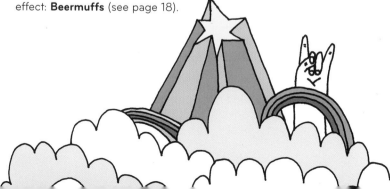

INCREASE YOUR TROOPS

You *could* sing alone. You do in the shower. But to get the most of your singing efforts, it's to your advantage to increase your karaoke army. Like making out, karaoke is better with more than one. Plus, karaoke is more rewarding when you can justifiably heckle someone because you actually know him. Otherwise, you'd just be That Crazy Guy At The Bar everyone tries to ignore.

A karaoke army is your personal cheerleading squad; even when you're really off-key. They'll go to the ends of the bar for you, especially if you've bought the last round. They'll even prevent you from singing Glenn Medeiros's "Nothing's Gonna Change My Love for You" a third time. And they don't just do it for you—their reputations are on the line too. They don't necessarily want people to know that they're with the guy who cries during the chorus of soft-rock ballads.

Your army will make venturing to new bars less intimidating. Someone in your group is bound to flirt with a cutie from the neighboring crew. Sparks will fly, shots will be downed, and soon enough, opposing teams will merge into one big party.

But recruitment won't be easy. Some people think karaoke is hard. Some think it's a kind of sushi roll. Karaoke conjures images of slurring drunks fighting over a mic. While there's some truth to all that (sushi aside), it's your job to convince people otherwise. Because no one should be above karaoke until they've tried. Once they do, they'll be fighting you for "nexts."

When faced with dissenters, whip the following nuggets out of your back pocket. Voilà: instant entourage.

COP-OUT: "I can't sing."

COMEBACK: "You mean, 'I won't sing.' Julie Andrews wasn't born a fabulous singing nun. Dean Martin wasn't born with a martini in one hand and a mic in the other. But they practiced, and you can too."

COP-OUT: "No, really. I have a horrible voice."

COMEBACK: "All the better. Look at all the mileage William Hung got out of his ***American Idol*** audition! Someone might film it with their camera phone, post it to YouTube, and you'll be famous!"

COP-OUT: "I don't want to make a fool of myself."

COMEBACK: "Change that 'fool' to 'cool'! Just do a Pat Benatar shoulder shimmy or the Axl Rose slither. You'll look totally hot and be the life of the party." (See page 68 for killer dance moves to teach your reluctant friends.)

COP-OUT: "There aren't any songs I like."

COMEBACK: "The songbook has four thousand songs. It's impossible not to like Cash or Bacharach or the Beatles or the new, improved Justin Timberlake. I just *dare* you to hate Prince circa *Purple Rain*. And did you notice that they have 'Achy Breaky Heart'? Here, let me sign you up for that right now."

CONTINUED...

COP-OUT: "I'm a real musician. And karaoke isn't real music."

COMEBACK: "Does being a real musician mean being a real snob? Karaoke is real people singing the soundtracks to their own lives. Now that's real." (Works best when followed by fierce drag queen–style Zorro snapping.)

COP-OUT: "Karaoke is so uncool."

COMEBACK: "'Cool' is about having a good time and not caring what other people think. Didn't your mom teach you this in high school?"

COP-OUT: "I'll only karaoke if I'm bombed."

COMEBACK: "Can I buy you a drink?"

KARAOKE BEERMUFFS

You'll find yourself wearing Beermuffs, a most flattering accessory, around the time you start slurring. Beermuffs distort and enhance your perception of bar events, particularly the quality of your own performance. Wearing Beermuffs may lead you to believe you sound, dance, and look far better than you actually do. If you're lucky, Beermuffs will prevent you from remembering the highlights of said performance. You'll be heartened to know that, having reached a comparable level of inebriation, your fans' hearing will be just as impaired as your own.

Those who claim to only reach karaoke enlightenment when sloshed use Beermuffs as a crutch. Beware: They're just trying to mooch drinks off you.

TEN REASONS KARAOKE IS BETTER THAN SINGING IN THE SHOWER

You've been singing naked for as long as you can remember. But doesn't it get lonely in there? Isn't it time to be, in the words of Billy Joel, movin' out? Here are ten reasons to dry off and get dressed.

1. You can get dates from karaoke.

2. Cuter people go to karaoke than go to your bathroom.

3. Your toothbrush isn't amplified.

4. Karaoke doesn't make your fingers prune up.

5. Your shower doesn't have an unlimited supply of gin and tonics.

6. Karaoke has an unlimited supply of the Carpenters.

7. You can't dance in the shower. Your mom says you might slip and crack your head open.

8. Karaoke will make you feel like an **American Idol**.

9. The shower will make you feel like a wet fish.

10. Shower acoustics actually really suck.

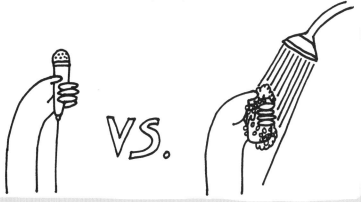

VS.

THE KARAOKE LIFE: A MANIFESTO

After the bar clears out and they've started flickering the lights, you're still in that deep groove. You hope the Bee Gees' "How Deep Is Your Love" never ends. Where to go from here? When you're this serious about singing, join the movement, embrace the fury, live the life. *The karaoke life.* Now take a pledge to make every floor a karaoke stage.

KARAOKE LIFE IS KARAOKE EVERY DAY.

It's about singing and more singing, and not just in the karaoke bar. Sing all the time, until you can't breathe.

KARAOKE LIFE IS SPONTANEOUS SINGING.

Sing at the supermarket. Sing on the train. Sing where it's least expected. Sing to your children. Sing to your mom. She will really appreciate it.

KARAOKE LIFE IS INFECTIOUS.

Singing is contagious. You may be the first to start, but the fever will spread.

KARAOKE LIFE IS SPIRITUAL.

Singing can bring you closer to the powers that be, be they David Bowie or otherwise divine.

KARAOKE LIFE IS UNADULTERATED BLISS.

Writhing on the floor and clutching the mic for dear life, sing because it feels good. With the melody soaring out of your body, you sing for *you*.

**SING IT LIKE YOU MEAN IT.
SING IT LIKE YOU OWN IT.
SING IT LIKE YOU'RE LIVING IT.
BECAUSE YOU ARE.**

CHAPTER 2

THE HISTORY

To be an aficionado, you have to know more than just how to harmonize "More Than Words" in the shower (although that's not a bad skill to have if you're expecting company in there). To be a real expert, you need a history lesson.

Who invented karaoke? Why is it rude to blink on stage? Where was the first karaoke bar in America? Are you even saying "karaoke" correctly? Answers to these mysteries lie ahead.

KARAOKE IS NOT JAPANESE FOR "DRUNK SINGING"

Is it *kala-okay, cara-okay*, or *carry-okie*? (Common misspellings include *kareoke, kareeokee, kareoky*, and *careoke*.) Actually, it depends where you are: "karaoke" is often pronounced in America as *carry-okie*, but sounds more like *calla-okay* in Japan. Like Nintendo or sukiyaki (which, by the way, is an excellent karaoke standard), karaoke is one of Japan's most universally understood terms. But contrary to popular belief, *karaoke* is not Japanese for "inebriated yodeling."

Karaoke is a combination of two words. *Kara* means "empty" and *oke* is short for *ōkesutora*, a word based on the English "orchestra." Put them together and you get "empty orchestra," or slang for prerecorded music replacing live music—think of cueing an iPod instead of hiring a live band for your house party. But don't think having an "empty" orchestra is a bad thing. Quite the contrary, karaoke has a full band sound. It's just that the musicians are invisible.

Typically, karaoke involves singing to prerecorded music (but see "Quirkyoke" on page 123 for variations on the standard). The songs are generally popular radio hits—by Madonna, Patsy Cline, Van Halen, or Bing Crosby for example—sung by amateurs at a bar. The singer makes a selection from a songbook, and the **KJ**, or **karaoke jockey**, cues it up. The singer then sings into a mic, and the performance blasts through a PA system. One key feature is the **lyrics teleprompter**. This monitor displays the lyrics in time with the music; the words change color when it comes time to sing them. The teleprompter makes it possible for people who don't know the lyrics to sing.

THE BATTLE FOR KARAOKE

You're not alone if you thought karaoke was a Japanese phenomenon. But that's not completely true. A few countries proudly claim to be the birthplace of karaoke. It emerged in a few different forms in the mid-1970s, most notably in the Philippines and, indeed, Japan. The Welsh also claim to have invented public singing, which they maintain is an early form of karaoke. While there is little proof of this, Wales gets extra credit for calling itself "The Land of Song."

BIG IN JAPAN

While it's more fun to believe that karaoke is an antiquated Kabuki ritual, the actual history has nothing to do with ritual and everything to do with bad singing. An early form of karaoke can be traced to the *utagoe kissa*, or singing cafés, of the early 1960s. But unlike the solo singer–focused karaoke, *utagoe kissa* goers sang in unison.

In 1971, a thirty-year-old Kobe keyboardist and vibraphone backup player became known for a unique gift: manipulating music to make the worst singer croon in tune. Needless to say, he was very popular. The man, Daisuke Inoue, was dubbed "The Human Karaoke Machine."

Inoue received so many requests to play his flattering renditions that he decided to create a machine version of himself. He combined a car stereo, a coin box, and an amp, creating the first coin-operated singing machine, which he called the "8-Juke." When the first eight machines sold instantly, he produced ten thousand more. What started out as a Band-Aid for bad singing become an instant hit.

At first criticized as being artificial and faddish, karaoke soon appeared in bars and hotels all over Japan. It has since become an integral part of Japanese social, business, and family life.

I took a car stereo, a coin box, and a small amp to make the karaoke. Who would even consider patenting something like that? — Daisuke Inoue, godfather of Japanese karaoke (who, incidentally, neglected to patent his genius invention)

THE HUMAN KARAOKE MACHINE
Daisuke Inoue is the underdog of karaoke. Adore him because:

★ In 1999, *Time* magazine named Inoue one of the twentieth century's "Most Influential Asians." *Time* noted that the singing machine had "helped liberate legions of the once unvoiced; as much as Mao Zedong or Mohandas Gandhi changed Asian days, Inoue transformed its nights."

★ In 2004, at Harvard University, Inoue was presented with the Ig Nobel Peace Prize, a joke award presented by real Nobel Prize winners. He was honored for "providing an entirely new way for people to learn to tolerate each other."

★ Inoue's life story is the subject of a Japanese biopic simply named *Karaoke*. The plump, round Inoue is played by a considerably taller, better-looking actor.

★ Inoue currently makes a living selling eco-friendly cockroach repellent for karaoke machines. According to him, "Cockroaches get inside machines, build nests, and chew on the wires."

THE FLIP SIDE

Though Inoue never filed a patent for his karaoke coin-op, losing his chance to cash in on a global success, another Asian inventor did. Filipino entrepreneur Roberto "Bert" Del Rosario developed and patented the "Sing-Along Machine" in 1975. Packaged as a "portable multipurpose machine," the Sing-Along came with a double to single tape deck, an amp, an optional tuner, and a mic mixer. Like Inoue's 8-Juke, the Sing-Along helped poor singers get on key.

Inoue and Del Rosario would not be the only inventors to claim firsts. When Del Rosario filed for the patent, a Chinese company sued Rosario, claiming to have invented something called the "Miyata Karaoke." Not much is known about this device.

So who is the father of karaoke? It's still unclear. But the Philippines' Supreme Court ruled that Del Rosario was the legal father, in that he was the first patent holder of karaoke machines.

THE PRIDE OF THE PHILIPPINES

To Filipinos, the **Magic Mic** is synonymous with national pride. A staple in Filipino homes worldwide, the Magic Mic is a self-contained karaoke system, with songs embedded on chips inserted into the mic. The Magic Sing catalog proudly features hits by Filipino songwriters and performers, traditional songs, and religious hymns.

The WOW Magic Sing Premium box carries the Filipino flag and the WOW Philippines pictures and logo. With this feature, people will definitely say, *"Ang ganda ng Pilipinas!"* ("How beautiful is the Philippines!" in Tagalog.) Wowmagicsing.com is the retail site for the Magic Mic.

Interestingly, the Magic Mic includes a foldout pamphlet on Filipino tourist destinations that, according to the Web site, "makes you a better-informed Filipino." Instead of videos, Magic Mic features scenes of Philippines tourist spots. No country has been more proud to rock the mic; Magic Sing is the official karaoke brand of the Philippines Department of Tourism.

KARAOKE FOR WORLD PEACE

In 2001, South Korea donated $900,000 in aid to North Korea, where the people suffer from severe food shortages and extreme weather. Included in the aid packages were not only 120 goats, 17,000 sets of underwear, and foodstuffs, but also 10 karaoke machines, programmed with 4,000 Western and South Korean pop songs. Organizers hoped that karaoke would contribute to inter-Korean reconciliation. I like to think it did.

EAST MEETS WEST

In the late '70s, karaoke gained wide acceptance not only in Japan but also in the rest of Asia—Taiwan, China, Korea, Thailand, Singapore, and the Philippines. Asians who left the motherland took karaoke wherever they settled. In the '90s, karaoke began popping up in Asian communities all over the United States, Europe, Canada, and Australia. As a rule of thumb, anywhere there's a Chinatown, Japantown, or Thaitown, there's sure to be karaoke.

But while singing, carousing, and boozing happen the world over, karaoke is practiced differently in the East and in the West. Here's a list of cultural differences that will make you want to rethink singing Tone Lōc's "Wild Thing" the next time you're in a Tokyo **karaoke box**.

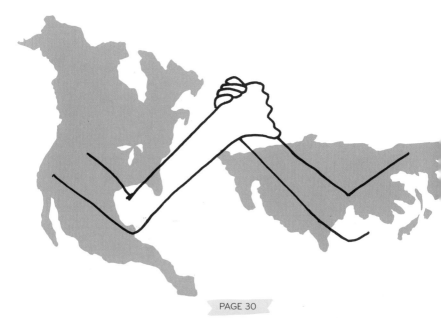

EAST **VS.** WEST

EAST

1. Practiced at home.

2. Practiced with friends. Also seen as a way to bond with family. The karaoke box acts as a second living room for young people in high-density cities.

3. Automated song systems (where patrons program their own songs) are most common.

4. The focus is on a solo performance. Group sing-alongs are rare and considered rude.

5. Irony is not encouraged. Asians just don't do "I'm Too Sexy" for laughs.

6. Karaoke is the center of activity at bars. Not Ms. Pac-Man.

7. The karaoke performance is taken very seriously and therefore rehearsed. In Japan, you can even take classes to help you improve your game.

WEST

1. Mostly sung at bars. Private rooms are not as popular in the West.

2. Practiced with acquaintances, friends, and coworkers.

3. KJ handles song requests and all activities. Automated systems are rare at karaoke bars.

4. Group sing-alongs are widely accepted. Singing in unison is a morale booster and is encouraged.

5. Spot-on irony is appreciated and even rewarded, as is Right Said Fred.

6. Karaoke is not the central activity in the barroom. It often shares real estate with pool, darts, and shuffleboard.

7. The West perceives karaoke as a jokey sport for people who want to embarrass themselves. But this book and aficionados like you are changing this perception as we speak—or rather, sing.

SINGING IS SERIOUS BUSINESS

In Japan, the most important business isn't conducted in boardrooms but under the glow of the **lyrics teleprompter**. Like the golf course for American execs, the karaoke room is where deals, networking, and promotions take place for the Japanese. If you want to climb the corporate ladder, singing is mandatory.

But you don't want to be caught stumbling over the first few lines of "I Wanna Sex You Up" in front of the boss. In Japan, men and women are expected to follow strict gender etiquette when it comes to karaoke. Men should stand with their feet shoulder width apart, with the mic in one hand and the cord in the other. Women have far more restrictions. Blinking, leaning against a wall, and putting a hand in your pocket are highly frowned upon. Holding the mic with two hands with a pinky lifted, afternoon-high-tea-style, is also taboo!

Here is a list of karaoke tips for young women just starting out in the Japanese workforce:

1. Listen respectfully to the singing of the boss.
2. Practice and be able to sing at least three duet songs so that you are able to accompany your boss on request.
3. Never pick a song your boss might pick (for he might not know many songs).
4. Avoid songs that are depressing or about separation and lost love.
5. Avoid songs that your boss may not know.
6. Avoid sexy songs that are likely to offend senior office ladies.
7. When not singing, be sure to maintain an awareness and express an interest in those around you.

(adapted from *Karaoke: A Global Phenomenon*, Zhou Xun and Francesca Tarocco)

THE KARAOKE WORLD CHAMPIONSHIPS: THE OLYMPICS OF SINGING

Asia and North America are not the only corners of the world where karaoke thrives; Finland, home of the **Karaoke World Championships**, is also a karaoke capital. Heidi Mattila, director of the KWC, talks about the Finnish love for singing and what it takes to win.

Q. How did you start the KWC?

A. KWC is a family-run business. It was my parents who "gave birth" to KWC. They had been organizing Finland's Karaoke Championships for many years, but when they found out that there was no world competition they decided to organize one in 2004, with representatives from seven countries. Now over thirty countries participate!

Q. Why is karaoke so popular in your country?

A. Karaoke is VERY popular; the reason is because Finnish people are quite shy and not extroverted. For example, it is unusual to speak to strangers. If you do, people think you are weird. When shy Finnish people start to karaoke, they come alive, finally allowed to show their feelings. And it doesn't matter how badly you sing—everyone will cheer you on. Karaoke lets the Finnish come out of their shells!

CONTINUED...

Q. What does it take to win KWC?

A. If you become your country's champion and win your way to KWC you need to 1) practice and practice and 2) choose songs that will fit your personality. You need to be able to sing five songs in different styles to show you can handle a range. You'll also need to sing all five perfectly, since all the points from each song are added together. Also, **stage presence** is very important. If you have a perfect voice but zero stage presence, it's not enough. It is important to charm the audience and jury. You need to make them feel *alive* when they're watching your performance.

Q. What are the best performances you have seen?

A. I've seen so, so many! But the ones I remember are two performances from KWC—by Uche Eke, KWC 2004 Male Champion, and Mark Wilson, KWC 2006 Male Champion. Uche sang Frank Sinatra's "Fly Me to the Moon" and it simply was something I enjoyed very much, made me feel like dancing!

When I found out that Mark was going to sing Céline Dion's "My Heart Will Go On," I thought "My God, I have never heard it sung by a man!" When he started singing it was something I did not expect to hear. He had such a clear voice that was perfect for that song. His performance gave me shivers and almost made me cry because it was so beautiful.

Q. Which countries have the best karaoke singers?

A. KWC champions so far have come from the United Kingdom, Malaysia, Ireland, Austria, Lebanon, and Australia. New countries are always entering, so for sure in the future there will be more countries with the world's best karaoke singers!

CHAPTER
3

RULE THE SCENE

Pull up a barstool and get comfy. It's time to get to know your new home away from home. Find out what those slips of paper are for and why it's mandatory to tip the KJ. Learn the subtleties of K'Etiquette so you never offend. Weigh the pros and cons of karaoke bars versus boxes, and how to deal with all the karaoke archetypes—both painful and pleasing—you'll encounter in the world. When you know what to expect, every bar will be your personal stage.

THE RITUAL

The holy act. It's just not karaoke unless these things happen:

1. Make a well-pondered selection from the songbook. Bacharach, Bon Jovi, Beyoncé, and Billy Ocean all look sweet, but choose your fave.

2. Write the name of the song, artist, and/or the corresponding song number on the song slip and hand it to the **KJ**. He winks at your good taste and enters the song in the queue.

3. Wait your turn. Sip your White Russian. Size up the competition. Glance at the screen to see your place in the queue.

4. Take the mic in one hand and the cord in the other. Scramble for the **lyrics teleprompter**, which is within eyeshot. The video begins and the words appear on the screen. They change color and...

5. Sing! Sing it like you mean it. Sing it like there's no second song!

THE SETUP

When going out to sing, you'll face one of two popular setups: the karaoke bar or the karaoke box. Here's what you can expect at each.

THE KARAOKE BAR

It's hard to find a bowling alley, lounge, or dive bar that doesn't have karaoke once a week. Karaoke's spread like wildfire on both coasts, to the South, and to the new hotbed of karaoke, the Pacific Northwest. Some places have a real stage, which separates the singer from the masses. Others relegate karaoke to just another barroom activity like darts or shuffleboard. If you have a problem sharing the stage with a Ms. Pac-Man machine, karaoke-only venues (offering singing every night of the week) have become popular, too (see "Legendary Karaoke Spots," page 140).

THE KARAOKE BOX

The box is the alternative for singers who would rather keep their talents among friends; it's like a singing hotel: You and your loudest friends can rent rooms with private systems by the hour. There's room service (food and drink) and an automated song select system, so anyone in your party can input music. This also means you can abort your boyfriend's ninth attempt at "Desperado" or that Wilson Phillips song no one will admit to picking. At the box, time is money, so sing only the best!

REMOTE CONTROL: CANCELING CRAP SONGS

It happens in private karaoke rooms. The premature aborting of a song can be downright offensive to the singing party, but can be justified when someone is really, really terrible. If your coworker can barely hum "I Wanna Dance with Somebody," you are in the right to slam the CANCEL button on the song remote. If you choose something everyone hates, expect to get vetoed. No one wants to spend his or her valuable box time (and money) listening to crap. The best part about singing in a box is that anyone—not just a KJ—has remote control.

BOX VS. BAR

It's up to you. While the shy and the mic-happy prefer the box, exhibitionists love the barroom stage. In fact, some bar purists don't think it's "real karaoke" unless you're working a crowd. They dare to refer to the box as "practice."

Box advocates, however, find the bar scene too unpredictable. They prefer to sing without the two-hour wait per song. Boxes are hugely popular in Asian communities, while the bar is the dominant form of karaoke everywhere else. Check the pros and cons and decide for yourself.

 THE BOX

More airtime. Start singing immediately. No more waiting for strangers to finish unbearable Matchbox Twenty songs!

The CANCEL button. Abort boring songs and bad singers with the all-powerful song remote.

Room service. Order drinks, chips, and tambourines from the comfort of the grimy couch. Never stand up again!

No public embarrassment. You're only embarrassing yourself in a room of familiar faces.

Less challenging. You're singing to the converted. You know your friends will still like you even if you suck.

Gross little rooms. A hallway lined with small musty rooms rented by the hour is not unlike a brothel.

Unchecked song selection. With no **KJ** to regulate things, an unmonitored **mic hog** could enter five *Oklahoma!* songs in a row.

The songbook smells like B.O.

THE BAR

⭐ **Even song rotation.** Song order at a bar has nothing to do with how fast you enter in songs. The **KJ** will make sure you don't clog the queue.

⭐ **A real captive audience.** What could be more exhilarating? You get to charm not just your five best friends but some totally cute stranger.

⭐ **Higher stakes.** Share the stage with strangers, you're forced to make your song the best.

⭐ **Waiting sucks.** On a crowded night, you'll sing once every three hours. Maybe.

⭐ **Unpredictable audience.** Is anyone listening? Some crowds are supportive, others are more concerned with the drink special. Captivating the crowd is no cakewalk.

⭐ **The songbook smells like B.O.**

TIP: THE EARLY BIRD SINGS MORE SONGS

If you're itching for more airtime at the bar, go early. Late afternoon and pre-dinner are optimal singing times. If you go to a crowded bar at prime time (8 P.M. or later), prepare to wait forty minutes to two hours per song. Instead, check out happy hour. Not only are the drinks cheap, most people don't sing in the daytime. And they're missing out. Try **karaoke boxes** for happy-hour rates, also.

THE ORIGIN OF KARAOKE VIDEOS

It wouldn't be classic karaoke without painfully outdated karaoke music videos. Some are filled with bland scenes of a couple holding hands. Some feature a pretty girl strolling through tourist spots, or female friends holding hands—not unusual in Asia, but interpreted as "lesbian" in the States. Some are "arty" while others have storylines. Most are just non sequiturs, like a video for Madonna's "La Isla Bonita" that features a couple walking through a snowy Russian tundra. Some *isla bonita.*

The cheesier videos originate from Asia. According to Kurt Slep, CEO of **Sound Choice,** while Asian companies produced song videos, European and American publishers chose not to, electing instead to focus attention on the music—no video, no pictures, just lyrics. His explanation is simple: since Americans grew up with elaborate MTV-style videos, "anything less ends up looking like . . . videos from karaoke songs." Since the music publishers won't allow the song to be storyboarded (a.k.a. matching the videos with the lyric content), karaoke videos are the result of pulled-together stock footage that wasn't recorded for the song. Which explains the frozen-over *isla bonita.*

THE LYRICS TELEPROMPTER

The teleprompter is what makes karaoke *karaoke* and not conventional singing. With the words and the rhythm, it lets everyone believe they can sing without any experience. It works like the sing-alongs of the 1950s; instead of a ball bouncing over the words, the lyrics change color when it's time to sing. On duets, the vocals are color-coded—for example, red for female and blue for male, or blue for singer one and yellow for singer two. The colors vary with different music publishers.

If you can only remember the part of the song that goes "Su-su-ssudio," even the teleprompter won't help your Phil Collins. But stellar singing doesn't happen naturally. It happens with practice and strategic song choice. The best karaokers don't just sing. They *live it.* And real life doesn't come with a teleprompter.

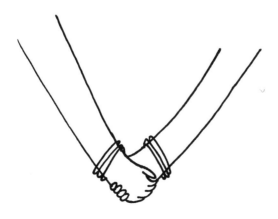

THE KARAOKE JOCKEY (KJ)

The KJ makes or breaks the experience. The KJ is the master of ceremonies, the ruler of the songbook, and the arbiter of song order disputes. Some KJs work at one bar, others freelance at various venues. A KJ is responsible for keeping the party going; he's also responsible for compiling an awe-inspiring song library.

As the controller of the spotlight, the KJ shouldn't hog the mic. He shouldn't sing more than one song every two hours. If he does, he's just as bad as Little Miss **Mic Hog**. A good KJ should also know how to rotate singers to keep the crowd happy and buying drinks. As mediator and entertainer, a KJ has a lot on his plate, so always tip well.

THE SONGBOOK

It's sticky, it smells, and it shouldn't be handled too closely. But, even if it's germ-infested, the songbook is the most important karaoke item besides the mic. If songs are the milestones in your adventures, the songbook is your roadmap. The book lets you know what's possible (yes! "Borderline" by Madonna!) and what's not (bummer, no "One" from *A Chorus Line*). You can judge a bar by the quality of the songbook, since a crappy selection will only inspire crappy singing.

A great song selection, however, does not just have the songs; it must have the best versions, too. For example, "I Say A Little Prayer" should never come up with a reggae beat. (It has.)

You can bet most popular songs have been karaokized (i.e., turned into karaoke instrumentals). That works to a fault; music publishers will karaokize anything popular. Enya's "Orinoco Flow" is in most songbooks, but is probably the worst song to sing—unless you sing Gaelic. Sometimes there's no rhyme or reason to what songs make it. While one bar's book has Engelbert Humperdinck in abundance, it could lack anything by a little foursome called the Beatles.

Regardless of what's in the books, it's impossible not to find something you can sing. And there's always the gold standard: Prince.

THE ARCHETYPES

Observe the Professional wringing his hands in his corner. See the Neophyte nervously downing shots. Watch the Thrasher growling like a pit bull. Loathe 'em or love 'em, you're singing with them—the native wildlife of the karaoke scene.

THE ASIAN LANGUAGE EXPERT

This guy speaks better Cantonese than the gangster running the karaoke bar. He's taught English in [insert any Asian country here] for at least three years. He's just "really into the culture," which includes karaoke. But he doesn't do Madonna, Garth Brooks, or anything else mainstream. He shows up at the **noraebang** with his well-culled list of Thai, Korean, and **Cantopop** hits and a minimum of two Asian girls.

THE THRASHER

This guy used to be in a band before he got cleaned up. But we're not sure that he cleaned up well. He still sings like it's the good ol' days. Like a pit bull, he's a breed that home insurance doesn't cover. He leaves holes in walls and flips off the authorities. A metalhead to the end, he's still living the glory years—Night Ranger, GN'R, Zeppelin, anything with high testosterone content. He can't sit still for any Bacharach or a really good ballad because of all the Ritalin.

THE AGING NEW WAVE FAN

You didn't know Depeche Mode cut a new album, nor did you listen to the B-sides of Erasure, a band whose albums you buried along with your neon tights and gummy bracelet collection. But the Aging New Wave Fan remembers it all. To him, New Order is alive and kicking, and he claims the new album is actually good. His set list is strictly classics: "Bizarre Love Triangle," Depeche, and anything that could be considered Eurotrash or gay. "The Promise" (When in Rome), "A Little Respect" (Erasure), and "Major Tom" (Peter Schilling) are all fair game.

THE NEOPHYTE

The prototypical Neophyte is Cameron Diaz from *My Best Friend's Wedding.* She's cute, charming, and tone-deaf. But everybody loves her dearly. She's got a lot of heart, so you don't have the heart to tell her that her "Vision of Love" was worse than the noise you hear when the radio dial is between stations. The neophyte has just started to karaoke and believes she can improve. Just let her believe. She's a valuable morale booster to any jaded scene.

THE LIFER

The Lifer says she went through her whole life without finding her one true love until she met karaoke. She's at the bars most weeknights even though she's a full-time nurse and mother of three. But what's admirable is that she makes time for her passion. While she'll admit that all the singing has affected her marriage, she'll also say karaoke has given her life new meaning.

THE SHOEGAZER

Generally shy, this person hates karaoke but loves music, which is the only reason she goes. She likes to see everyone else enjoy themselves but recoils when she gets handed the mic. Her friends are fanatics, which is why she is a bar staple. But she doesn't like the way her voice sounds, or how she looks onstage, and claims she can't remember lyrics. Eventually the list of excuses wears thin, and she'll break down with enough tequila.

THE PROFESSIONAL

The classically trained Professional has had fourteen years of voice lessons and was the understudy for Raoul in the local production of *Phantom*. He doesn't normally karaoke but he can let loose, and knows he'll have everyone eating out of his hand. It's an unfair advantage, like playing Little League with Barry Bonds. He may put everyone to shame, but at least he's a great example to aspire to.

THE MOR FAN

This person doesn't understand the makings of a good karaoke song, which explains his taste for Middle of the Road (MOR), those forgettable adult contemporary classics mostly from the '90s—Gin Blossoms, Hootie, Counting Crows—and, more recently, John Mayer and Coldplay. The MOR fan is actually a really nice guy. But nice guys finish last, especially if they prefer singing "You're Beautiful."

THE UNWORTHY MIC HOG

The Unworthy Mic Hog takes the stage. Again. It was OK at 5:00 when the bar was empty and no one had to listen to his off-key, creepy rendition of "Mack the Knife." But now it's 8:00 and the place is packed. You start to think he's paid off the **KJ** to delete everyone else's songs. He's a big burly guy, and you're intimidated. Moreover, you're annoyed. You can't believe he's singing "Like a Virgin"—without irony.

THE MIC HOG (FEMALE VERSION)

A modern pop queen, she doesn't know any music pre–Spice Girls. She's not a bad singer. You know she practices her Kelly Clarkson every morning. You admire her enthusiasm, but there's such a thing as too much. A single tween-pop song would be kind of cute, but like a venti Frappuccino, no one should have more than one. Unfortunately, she's entered in the next five.

K'ETIQUETTE

Etiquette is more than "don't throw up on the mic" or "don't hump the wall." Most bars are haunts for regulars. Think of it as a nature reserve—don't litter and put everything back where you found it. You're not going to be welcomed back if you don't respect the rules. And, worse, you'll only hear crickets when you sing.

Follow the Golden Rule. Cheer for others as you'd want them to cheer for you.

Be a good sport. Karaoke is not about winning or losing. Save that pressure for the World Championships.

Don't hog the mic. Just because you can sing doesn't mean you should. Again.

Don't repeat songs. You'll just look like a biter.

Don't crash the stage or sing along to others' solos. Don't sing on mic #2 uninvited!

Don't hijack other people's songs. This is terrible form unless they've left the bar or made a pass at your significant other.

Don't throw a fit. Don't go ballistic if you don't have the crowd's full attention. You have to earn it.

Don't fight over song order. Solve all disputes over shots. Soon you won't remember what you were fighting about.

Don't be too hard on yourself. By the next song, people will already have forgotten that your voice cracked like a prepubescent boy's.

Don't act like a prima donna. Reality check: If you were really that good you'd be headlining *Chicago* and not Palos Verdes Bowl on Friday nights.

Tip the KJ well. It's hard work rallying you hooligans.

Don't take yourself too seriously. Remember, it's karaoke!

CHAPTER 4

SING LIKE A PRO

The heart of karaoke is a lovely singing voice. But most of us weren't blessed with heavenly pipes. Some can barely get through "Happy Birthday." Singing is a learned skill. This chapter will show you that your voice is an instrument you can fine-tune. Make it pitch-perfect or ridiculously ironic. But most important, learn how to choose songs that will make you look good. Good karaoke happens when you pick songs that highlight your strengths, be they screaming, rapping, yodeling, or operatic vibrato.

MASTERING THE COVER SONG

Karaoke is all about mastering the cover song. Your performance is not a world premiere; someone famous already sang it first. It's your turn to do it justice (without all those computer programs that smooth out vocal imperfections—like Britney uses).

Singing a well-known song is a tall order. You're up against history; people remember the original. Everyone recalls just how Kim Carnes growls when she sings, "She's got Bette Davis eyes . . ." Your version will inevitably be compared to hers, growl or not. But you *can* outdo Miss Carnes with one of the following techniques.

HIGH FIDELITY
SINGING SKILL: HIGH
PREPARATIONS: HIGH
REWARD: HIGH

This is a rendition so "real" that the audience will think Belinda Carlisle is in the house. Remember, when people see their favorite bands in concert, they expect to hear the songs exactly the way they sound on the album; people like what they already know. And they obviously won't know you, but they *will* know Belinda, so skillful impersonation is a safe bet. It'll show you're disciplined—that you've listened to the original probably too many times.

To get the highest fidelity, study each quiver in Belinda's "I Get Weak." Try closing your eyes and listening to the original. Many, many times. Tape record yourself **a cappella**, and then play it back. Listen to your vocal inflections. Then ask yourself the big question: "Am I Belinda yet?" To answer yes, you have to get every last "w-w-w-w-w-w-eak" note down.

IRONY
SINGING SKILL: *NEGLIGIBLE*
PREPARATIONS: *MEDIUM*
REWARD: *HIGH*

So you're cheeky. And you're kind of a bastard. You can't sing, but you want to try Dan Hill's "Sometimes When We Touch," which is a parody of itself. Irony is difficult to pull off, but it can be done with the right song. The right songs take themselves very seriously, and are often sung by a musician who takes him- or herself seriously. John Mayer, Céline Dion, and Richard Marx all qualify.

Once you pick your victim, you'll have to decide how to sing it. Falsetto? Screaming punk rock–style? Rap? Doo-wop? Doing a poorly sung version of the original (in a serious tone) can be ironic enough. Whatever style you choose, stay in character. The best irony is deadpan. Don't lapse into uncontrollable giggles, even if you're a husky construction worker crooning "I Will Always Love You." You didn't see Whitney crack a smile performing it in *The Bodyguard,* did you? You'll break the mood and any spell you've cast on your audience.

SPONTANEITY
SINGING SKILL: MEDIUM/LOW
PREPARATIONS: NONE
REWARD: HIGH

A seasoned performer wings it. It's how professionals keep live shows interesting night after night. The expert winger can make up alternate lyrics for "Bust a Move" or a scat riff to the Nissan commercial song on the spot. He can get the grannies in the back to salsa dance. He's unforgettable. His performance is not just about the singing itself but about interacting with the crowd. Winging it requires equal parts self-assurance and shamelessness. It's hard to do a Hanukkah version of Mariah's "All I Want for Christmas" with self-doubt. It takes improvisational skills for which hip-hop MCs, method actors, and teachers all have a knack.

You may want to start small, calling out to a cute stranger to sing with you. But eventually you should use everything in the room in your routine. Pole dance with the pillars. Do a Fred Astaire flying heel kick off the bar counter. Get the waitress to hold the mic while you give that fireman a lap dance. Let your instincts guide you.

BEWARE OF GROUP KARAOKE

Late into the evening, karaoke can devolve into a cacophonous caravan. **Group karaoke** (singing with two or more, duets excluded) happens when a group of friends too drunk to know better storms the stage. The night might start off slow. But as people grow drunker and more restless waiting their turn, they'll sing to anything, even sans mic. That's the point at which karaoke becomes a messy group sing-along.

When the whole house sings Billy Joel's "The Longest Time" by heart, it's an awesome feeling. It demonstrates that music really can unite the world. But if you're a career **karaoker**, you'll probably find group karaoke annoying. With that many voices, your talent will get lost in the mix. Group karaoke is a sign of amateur karaoke skill, which is not to say it's a bad thing. Pros tend to steer clear because they want the attention for themselves.

STRATEGIES FOR THE GOOD, THE BAD, AND THE TONE-DEAF

What's your talent? Play it cool no matter how good or crappy you are. Figuring out how well you sing is like figuring out how hot you are—you can tell by the looks on other people's faces. If you're still not sure if you sound more like Miss Piggy than Patsy Cline, a good way to gauge is to pay close attention to your audience. Are they yawning, blinking too much, or hanging on to your every move? Are they busy texting or bopping? The ultimate praise is when your singing grabs the attention of bar employees. The waitresses and the bartender have seen enough karaoke for a lifetime. But if your singing makes them smile, you're doing something right.

Once you know your skills, here are some strategies for the good, the OK, and the really bad.

PRODIGY

DESCRIPTION: Why even sing with the masses? Go back to Broadway or wherever you came from. You've been upstaging bad singers everywhere since childhood.

ANALYSIS: If you can sing like an angel, you don't have to do much. Everyone loves you, and you get compliments up the wazoo. But even perfection can get boring. Good singers know how to showcase their talent by mixing things up.

ADVICE: Change it around. Mix in more upbeat and less dramatic songs. Skip "Memory" from *Cats* for Duran Duran's "Rio." Pick a song everyone can groove to. Singing beautifully every time will make people feel bad that they're not you.

PASSABLE

DESCRIPTION: You love music and can hold a tune. Your hard work, young understudy, will pay off.

ANALYSIS: You're not bad. You'll sing in key and know the songs by heart. What you lack in skill you make up in accuracy. But unfortunately, it's the really good and really terrible who leave an impact.

ADVICE: Really work it. The only way is up. Even if your pitch isn't perfect, you can fake it with the right songs. Even if you can't hit the highs, the crowd will see that you have heart.

VOCALLY CHALLENGED

DESCRIPTION: Poor thing, you've got a tin ear.

ANALYSIS: You didn't listen to music as a kid. How else can you explain singing Tom Jones' "Sex Bomb" in one monotonous note? You've made something that was once sultry as appetizing as stale toast.

ADVICE: Homework is mandatory. But for now the path of irony will be your only salvation. Work up a routine that's so bad it's good. You'll be known as that really awful girl whom everyone loves. At least people won't forget you. See, you're sort of lucky that way.

CHAPTER
5 GET
WIN AFF

Everybody loves a rock star. That's why they get so many groupies. Similarly, everybody loves a karaoke star. The bright lights, the way your hair looks backlit on stage, the music. . . it's all pretty tantalizing. When you're awesome at karaoke, people will want to know you. They will buy you drinks. You'll gain the social status you never had in high school. You'll be a superstar (at least within earshot).

But achieving karaoke stardom isn't all about being *Idol*-worthy. You don't even need to know how to sing. To make it, you need to know how to work everything else—from mastering **stage presence** to being a social force offstage. If it were just about singing, karaoke wouldn't be half as much fun. And there'd be no hope for most of us.

KARAOKE BETTER IN FIVE STEPS

Why be mediocre when you can rule? You can always karaoke better. Here's how.

STEP 1: KNOW YOUR SONGS!

This is Number One, but the one that is least followed. Stumble over the words and you'll be booed. Blank out and people will wonder why they should be staring at you and not their medicating glass of Scotch and soda. When your eyes are glued to the **lyrics teleprompter**, people can tell you don't know what you're doing. So practice and know the music!

STEP 2: PREPARE.

Prepare your **set list** (see Chapter 6). Floss. Smell like roses. Dress to impress. And don't over-booze. You won't be able to pull off the charming drunkard act right away—that will take years of studying Dean Martin. But if you prepare, you should be able to manage the mic in one hand and a half-drunk martini in the other.

STEP 3: BE YOURSELF.

Your personal style is how you do what you do—your delivery, your song, and your **stage presence**. It's the way you exude *you* (which hopefully doesn't involve any odd smells). But don't be afraid to do what comes to mind. Doing "Paradise City" as a ballad can make you an innovator. And the fact that you can belly dance to any song, well, that's something that's purely you. Cultivate your personal stage style. And don't be afraid to have a shtick.

STEP 4: WORK THE ROOM.

Meet new people. Buy drinks. Remember names. Karaoke is based on reciprocity, so people will return the favor when you cheer. And since everyone's an amateur doing it for the love, karaoke crowds tend to be friendly. We're all embarrassing ourselves (some more than others), so it's easy to bond with strangers. Take advantage.

STEP 5: SHOW YOUR PASSION.

Boring people have no interests, and passionate people deeply love at least one thing, whether it's stamp collecting, eBay, or kickball. Make karaoke *your* thing. The fact that you did the caterpillar on the filthy barroom floor means you're serious. And if you couldn't hit the last five (or the next ten) notes of that Neil Diamond song, at least you have passion. Oddly, most people don't.

WHAT TO WEAR

Approach dressing for karaoke like dressing for Halloween—be whoever you want. There's no lace bustier or shredded T-shirt too taboo. You're guaranteed an audience for at least three minutes and twenty-six seconds, so indulge your wildest fashion whims. And remember, the more costume-y, the better. Singing newsboy? Mop-top rocker? Nothing is too much. You're dressing to impress—or at least leave an impression.

STYLE ICONS

⭐ Marianne Faithfull, Rolling Stones groupie (poet blouse, beaded hippie jewelry, long flared pants)

⭐ Ren Faire Wench (poet blouse, tights, winged jodhpur-type pants)

⭐ Joan Baez and Bob Dylan–style hippie flower child (grimy T-shirt, military fatigues, flowy gauzy ethnic top)

⭐ George Michael (white shorts and neon "Choose Life" T-shirt from the "Wake Me Up Before You Go-Go" video)

⭐ David Bowie (androgynous clothes, unitard, low-cut tight top, platform shoes)

⭐ The Rat Pack: Frank Sinatra, Sammy Davis Jr., Dean Martin (fitted blazer and skinny tie, dress shoes, crisp button-down shirt, and hat)

WHAT TO BRING

You can never be too rich, too thin, or too prepared for karaoke.

BRING ♥

- ☐ DOG-EARED COPY OF *HIT ME WITH YOUR BEST SHOT!*
- ☐ SET LIST
- ☐ BREATH MINTS OR GUM FOR INTIMATE DUETS
- ☐ PLENTY OF CASH TO TIP THE KJ
- ☐ BEST SMILEY FACE
- ☐ BUSINESS CARDS, WITH STAGE NAME AND CONTACT INFO
- ☐ ASPIRIN, FOR BAD SINGING (NOT YOURS)
- ☐ PEN FOR SONG REQUESTS WHEN ONE AT THE BAR DISAPPEARS
- ☐ MP3 RECORDER FOR PLAYBACK OF TRIUMPHANT PERFORMANCES
- ☐ GREAT GROUP OF PEOPLE

SUNDAY I'M IN LOVE

AVOID

- ☐ FOOD AND DRINK WITH DAIRY. MILK CAUSES EXCESS MUCUS IN YOUR THROAT. THE NORMAL AMOUNT OF MUCUS YOU HAVE IS FINE
- ☐ COFFEE, RED WINE, CHEWING TOBACCO, OR ANYTHING THAT DISCOLORS YOUR MOUTH
- ☐ CIGARETTES, THEY DEHYDRATE YOU
- ☐ ALCOHOL. IF YOU ARE SERIOUS ABOUT SINGING WELL, BOOZE DEHYDRATES YOU TOO
- ☐ DEDICATIONS TO ANYONE DEAD OR DYING
- ☐ WHINING

GET DATES AND WIN AFFECTION
THE ROCK STAR EFFECT

Karaoke brings people together, but not just on the stage. In the words of Olivia Newton-John, "We're talking horizontally!" While the orthodox consider it uncouth to elicit dates from karaoke, it's a legitimate social practice. With all that dancing and singing, karaoke is a postmodern mating ritual. You're an immediate heartthrob if you can channel Elvis Costello: a meta-star. Case in point:

I once dated a guy I met at karaoke. He was the world's biggest dork—a thirty-three-year-old virgin and a Computer Science PhD. But his karaoke skills influenced me to date him even though we were pretty incompatible. He did a spot-on "Welcome to the Jungle." To this day, no man can karaoke that song for me. It's off-limits.
—Jennilyn, 28, Allentown, Pennsylvania

When good karaoke gets you booty, it's called the **Rock Star Effect**. Here are tips to help you get some.

DUETS

Two *can* become one. Singing a duet shows that you can be half of a whole. Look, you can share! Once you sing "Always" by Atlantic Starr ("Come with me my sweet, let's go make a family"), it'll be obvious that you're capable of deeply loving someone, at least for the duration of the song. That should be long enough to secure the booty.

♡ CALL ME ♡
476 - 8000

DEDICATIONS

If you've got designs on someone, there's no better way to get their attention than serenading him or her, *Top Gun*–style. Cheesy, yes. But effective (it worked for Maverick). You could also serenade an unlikely target, like the octogenarian bartender. Certainly someone besides the bartender will find you cute enough to take home.

MUTUAL HUMILIATION

Singing in public creates a deep social bond of shared embarrassment. We're all trying, right? Swoop in at the low moments. Console that lonely young man in the corner. Tell him his Jon Secada wasn't really so bad. Sympathize, and you'll gain his confidence *and* phone number.

COSTUMES

Wear tight clothes (it's not as tasteless as it sounds). Leave those jeans that give you "mom butt" at home. Frumpy duds will send anyone who might have sexed you up packing. Instead, flaunt and flatter. Squeeze into Lenny Kravitz–worthy skinny pants, even if you can't button the top. Your lower half doesn't need to breathe, and your butt will look *so* good. (Men, this applies to you, too!)

TIP: USE A STAGE NAME

It's a good idea to christen your singing alter ego. Unless your real name is as melodic as Winona, Elvis, or Rick James, you need a more theatrical moniker. If you're feeling uninspired, try the following formula to get your wheels turning: combine the first name of your favorite singer with the name of your favorite cocktail (Dixie Manhattan has a nice ring to it, no?). Write it on the song slip you hand to the KJ. And when the KJ calls out "Midnight Maelstrom," remember that it's actually you!

SHOULD I STAY OR SHOULD I GO NOW?

Are you cool under pressure or do you turn into a hothead when things don't go your way? Test your singing social smarts.

1. You put in your request over two hours ago. People who arrived after you have already finished singing their Avrils, Madonnas, and U2s. You:
- a) know the KJ is swamped and have some sympathy. You ask him politely when he will play your song and if he needs a drink.
- b) yell at the KJ for shafting you. And then storm out.
- c) steal someone else's song. The KJ was clearly ignoring you and you're never going back there again.
- d) have another drink.

2. You're two songs away and you realize that the man before you has also requested "Time After Time." You:
- a) sing it anyway. Hey, he doesn't own the song.
- b) leave in a huff. Cyndi is and always will be yours only!
- c) ask the KJ to switch to Heart's "Magic Man." It's harder but you're up for the challenge.
- d) pout and worry, wondering if you'll be judged against his rendition.

3. The party in the next booth has decided to relive their frat days. They drink, yell, and make "whoot whoot whoot" grunts. They don't care about singing or anybody else. You worry your "Blue Bayou" will be lost in the fray. You:
- a) try to ignore them, though your patience wears thin. You might have to smack one of them with a mic soon.
- b) leave the bar. You don't tolerate riffraff like that.

c) dedicate the next song to the Neanderthals in the back. You're glad they can stand upright now.
d) have another drink and tip the KJ. He then asks the gentlemen to keep their horsing around to a minimum. This is a karaoke establishment, after all!

4. **You're up next. After too many mojitos, you can barely remember your last name, let alone the words to "Suspicious Minds." You:**
a) look at your driver's license. That's your name, isn't it?
b) get on stage anyway and add in a bit of "Can't Take My Eyes Off of You." They seem to go well together.
c) throw your best Westsi-i-i-de! signs.
d) all of the above.

5. **Your ex shows up with a hot date. Things ended badly between you two and you've had more than your share of screwdrivers. You:**
a) dedicate this next one to the spineless grinch in the back. You rile up everyone in the bar to sing Kelly Clarkson with you. "Since you been gone, I can breathe for the first time..."
b) head to the bathroom and cry.
c) head to the stage and request "I Will Survive."
d) have another drink.

---

1. a) KJs do get swamped, especially if the house is packed. They don't need people yelling at them or pilfering other people's songs—if you do, you'll never sing in that joint again. Next time, arrive early and get your songs in before the masses get there. **2. c)** Show some courtesy. Don't upstage the previous singer—he got to it first. No one wants to listen to the same thing twice. Even if you think yours will be better, just let it lie. **3. d)** Let the KJ deal with losers. You can yell and make a fuss about them, but it's still not your domain. The KJ is the one responsible for keeping things running smoothly, so let him tell the fellas to pipe down. **4. d)** At this point, there's not much you can do. A gangsta "Suspicious Minds" is better than nothing. In your intoxicated state you think you sound really, really good... **5. c)** As tempting as choice A sounds (your heart is in the right place), after a breakup it's important to keep your dignity intact—even at karaoke. So don't let this surprise appearance kill your buzz. Sing "I Will Survive" and show that you can go on very happily without him.

YOU CAN DANCE: THE MOVES

If you're up there with your arms at your side, you'll look like a closed clamshell. Stage performance is a full-body expression. So do a few stretches and let loose. Let the music move you. Like Quiet Riot says, "Cum on, feel the noize." Feel it!

TIPS FOR GETTING FOOTLOOSE

Move like your audience is nearsighted. Go big. Exaggerate your moves. If your jazz hands look weak from two feet away, they'll just look like shaky coffee hands from the back of the bar.

Don't stand in one place. The statue thing gets monotonous, so cover ground. Size up the stage and then travel.

Use the right moves for the right music. The Jackson Five Head Jive might work for disco, Motown, and funk, but it does not work for Avril Lavigne.

Avoid *American Idol*–style hand grabs. You know, the one where it looks like you're reaching up to an imaginary bird, pulling it down, and then crushing it. To death.

Here are a few expert dance moves to get you started. Inspired by the best performers, these moves were adapted for karaoke by our in-house choreographer, Mirra Fine*.

PEEKABOO

Create mystery. At the beginning, stand with your back facing the audience. Then sharply turn your head over your left or right shoulder, making eye contact with your fans as you do. Very Supremes.

GENRE: WORKS WITH ALL
DIFFICULTY: EASY

HIP NUDGE

Bump it, you jazzy thing. Stand with your back to the audience and shake your hips to the beat. Shrug both shoulders and arms up and down. If you like, you can alternate between two styles. Jazz style is performed with Bob Fosse jazz hands (with fingers spread apart, wave your hands in small movements). Funk style is the same motion, but with your arms closer to your side. Finger snapping is optional but recommended. To get your party started, the Hip Nudge can be done before a Peekaboo.

GENRE: WORKS WITH ALL
DIFFICULTY: EASY

THE MIDDLE SCHOOL

This is that stationary dance move you did in junior high when you didn't know how to dance. But if you exaggerate it into a semi-plié, it works for the stage. Step together, clap, and then step apart and clap. Repeat.

GENRE: MOST, BUT WORKS BEST ON "LIKE A PRAYER"
DIFFICULTY: EASY

JACKSON FIVE HEAD JIVE

A great head move, the Jackson Five can do it in unison. The Jackson Five Head Jive has three positions. Bounce your head to the left, then dip it forward to the middle, and bounce to the right. Your head should be writing a soft lowercase "m" above your shoulders.

GENRE: MOTOWN, FUNK, FAST POP
DIFFICULTY: EASY

THE OPERATOR

Made famous by Mariah, it's performed with the most dramatic songs ("I'll Be There," "Vision of Love"). Hold the

CONTINUED...

mic in one hand and half of your imaginary headphones in the other. Then wave your headphone hand in midair, like you're operating a switchboard. Make your switchboard moves correspond with the music. Include the Turtleneck if you're feeling extra diva-ish.

GENRE: BRING-DOWN-THE-HOUSE SONGS

DIFFICULTY: THE MOVE IS EASY. BUT YOU HAVE TO BE DOING SOME MARIAH-QUALITY SINGING TO MERIT THIS MOVE.

TWITCHING FUNK

This is out-of-rhythm twitching that resembles a robot malfunctioning. It's a classic nerd dance: think Urkel, or Screech from *Saved by the Bell*. Gripping the mic tightly (because it could fly off), sharply jerk your entire body with the beat. Now sharply twitch without the beat. You can twitch over a lot of ground and will probably break something. But it works for irony's sake.

GENRE: ALL

DIFFICULTY: EASY FOR EVERYONE EXCEPT THE EXPERIENCED DANCER, WHO'D HAVE A HARD TIME TRYING TO LOOK THAT BAD.

THE SHOOP AND THRUST

For the Shoop, curl both arms in an ice cream–scooper shape, then scoop both arms and pelvis forward. Works well with "The Shoop Shoop Song (It's In His Kiss)" or any other '60s girl-group song. The next move, the Thrust, highlights the pelvis and is therefore racier. With the same curled arms, scoop your pelvis outwards while drawing your arms in, for that "uh!" effect. For best results, crescendo with a finger snap.

GENRE: DISCO, DANCE, FUNK

DIFFICULTY: MEDIUM

THE TURTLENECK

This move is for "head only" dancers who refuse to move the rest of their bodies. Sometimes known as "the Stevie Wonder," the Turtleneck is done by moving your head in varying degrees from left to right.

GENRE: FUNK, SOUL
DIFFICULTY: MEDIUM

KISSING THE FLOOR

When you're cheek to cheek with linoleum, you mean it. Inspired by the author's friend who performed a rolling floor tumble while singing "Hazard" by Richard Marx, this move can pump up the drama. It can make a mediocre song—like Bryan Adams' "(Everything I Do) I Do It for You"—come alive. And if you stay on the floor for the entire song, everyone will know you value a good show over hygiene.

GENRE: DRAMATIC BALLADS, SOFT ROCK
DIFFICULTY: MEDIUM

THE SHIMMY

It looked great on Pat Benatar and her tattered lady prostitute gang shaking their top parts in the "Love Is A Battlefield" video. It can work for you too, breasts or no breasts. Shake your shoulders from the front to the back, while keeping your head still. Imagine you're trying to shake those peaches off the tree without breaking the branch. Keep your arms open (and almost dead) at the sides, because the action will come from your chest. This can be done while traveling forward, when you're about to go *apeshit* on your pimp.

GENRE: VENGEFUL FEMME ROCK
DIFFICULTY: MEDIUM

CONTINUED...

SWINGING JAZZ SQUARE

Large full-motion arm swings and a stationary running motion accompany this move. Most ideal (and cheesy) when a couple singing a duet like "We Go Together" from *Grease* do the Swinging Jazz Square facing each other.
GENRE: SHOW TUNES, JAZZ, BIG BAND
DIFFICULTY: HARD

THE SWAYZE

In the finale of *Dirty Dancing,* Patrick Swayze leads his scruffy gang of dancers/waitstaff in a "let's show them!" dance: they all bend down, snap their fingers, and do a "traveling move" (walking and dancing). It's so much cooler than the ballroom dancing that the snooty resort patrons do.
GENRE: JAZZ, FUNK, OLDIES
DIFFICULTY: HARD

*Mirra Fine has been shaking her lovely thing for the past twenty years. Her credentials include "being the best dancer at any club or house party." She received a karaoke machine from her parents for her bat mitzvah and lives in New York City.

WHAT IT TAKES TO WIN A KARAOKE COMPETITION

Once you've perfected your routine, it's time to share your talents with the greater karaoke community. But in the career circuit it takes more than intimate knowledge of Bon Jovi to win. The judges base decisions on five performance qualities. The following guidelines come straight from the **Karaoke World Championship**'s USA handbook. Study and integrate them into your next performance.

VOICE QUALITY

- The quality and individual characteristics of the voice
- Dynamic range, including loud and soft
- Tonal color range—when singing smoothly here and gravelly there
- Strength and range of voice

PITCH (INTONATION AND PITCH CONTROL)

- Awareness of the intended key
- How accurately the singer harmonizes with the music
- Select use of vibrato, which is often overused

PHRASING

- Emotional expression
- Articulation: how well the audience can understand your words
- Awareness of the rhythmic style of the piece
- Staccato and legato sung correctly

STAGE PRESENCE

- Facial expression and body gestures
- Command of the audience through eye contact
- Appearance of confidence and relaxation on stage
- Costume or dress appropriate to represent the nation

AUDIENCE

- Entertainment value, overall performance
- Audience reaction, loudness of applause

SECRETS OF A KARAOKE WORLD CHAMPION: SAMANTHA SAYEGH, WINNER OF THE FIRST KARAOKE WORLD CHAMPIONSHIPS, 2004

Age: 25
Country: Lebanon
Occupation: Archaeology student, aspiring professional singer

Q. When did you first begin to karaoke?

A. I started singing at thirteen and worked on my voice in a polyphonic choir as soprano soloist for almost ten years. At that time, I did karaoke for pleasure at pubs. Karaoke was very popular in Lebanon in the early '90s.

Q. Have you had professional voice training?

A. No. I started working on my voice at the choir. Through the years I learned to know my voice. The voice is a muscle that you have to work out. I am still learning breathing and singing techniques for different music in different languages—English, French, Arabic, and Spanish.

Q. What makes a great karaoke singer?

A. A great karaoke singer should know that a karaoke competition is not only a singing competition. Therefore, other than the voice, a singer should have a good **stage presence** and interaction with the audience, in addition to a variety of music styles. A great performance should also have a good sound system, a good karaoke version of the song, stage presence, and of course a good voice!

Q. What are some of your favorite songs to sing?

A. "(You Make Me Feel Like) A Natural Woman" by Aretha Franklin, "Je T'aime" by Lara Fabian, and "Hero" by Mariah Carey.

Q. What is your advice to those who want to win karaoke competitions?

A. Choose good songs that suit your voice. Don't make the classic mistake of choosing songs you like to listen to that might not suit you. You need to know your songs very well, and not read the lyrics from the monitor during the performance! And most of all, you need to enjoy it!

CHAPTER 6

Which songs are unmistakably you? Which songs make you feel alive? Which ones do you never get sick of? This chapter will help you cull your favorites into a killer **set list**. The hard part is learning how to whittle down your list to songs that showcase your talent (or lack thereof) and, more important, make you look good. After all, the goal is to karaoke better than everyone else. To achieve this, you need to remember one thing: You can't sing every song perfectly, but you can sing songs that are perfect for you.

WHY A SET LIST?

Everyone has favorites, but determining which are best suited for your skills is the key to success. You may love the way Air Supply's high notes sound, but your rendition could fall flat. But the worst is when you pick up the mic for a Police tribute and realize you only know the part that goes, "De do do, de da da da, is all I want to say to you."

Unless you're forced to play Kamikaze (see page 133), you should tailor a set list of personal classics. A set list is traditionally a list of songs a band will perform in its live set. Here, they are songs for your own set. Set list songs should be ones you not only adore but can walk through blind. You should be able to perform them **a cappella** if need be. Remember, a true karaoke star doesn't need expensive equipment, great shower acoustics, or reverb; he or she just needs a good memory, tons of practice, and a well-curated set list.

YOUR SECRET WEAPON: YOUR JUHACHIBAN

You *cannot* sing everything. The best karaoke happens when you know how to pick your personal best, or your *juhachiban*. Meaning "eighteen" in Japanese, *juhachiban* is slang for "the one song you are the very best at singing." It's *the* song you were born to sing. And when you sing it, it shows. Your *juhachiban*, however, is not necessarily that one song where you can hit all the high notes, or even that favorite you've been singing since grade school. It's the song that you feel good singing, because it sums up *you* in a song.

YOUR SONGS

Your set list is like a room full of your oldest, dearest friends. They've stayed with you for years, so treat them lovingly and with respect. These are the songs that make you feel good. You know all their best features: the catchy chorus, the glorious bridge, and the long yodel at the end. They may be songs you can sing really well, or just love to hear coming out of your mouth. No idea where to start building yours? Here are the set lists of a few veterans.

RAINA (THAT'S ME!), NEW YORK, NEW YORK

With favorites and songs I'm able to sing well, my set list features female pop vocals and standards from my parents' generation, like "Superstar."

1. "Superstar," The Carpenters
2. "Gloria," Laura Branigan
3. "Since U Been Gone," Kelly Clarkson
4. "Blue Bayou," Linda Ronstadt
5. "Voices Carry," 'Til Tuesday
6. "I Get Weak," Belinda Carlisle
7. "Eye in the Sky," The Alan Parsons Project
8. "All Time High," Rita Coolidge
9. "Torn," Natalie Imbruglia
10. "Reminiscing," Little River Band
11. "Always," Atlantic Starr
12. "Danke Schoen," Wayne Newton
13. "We Belong," Pat Benatar

NICK, NEW YORK, NEW YORK

Nick's crowd-pleasers Rock with a capital "R." Especially Bon Jovi. And anything by Joan Jett is gold. Nick knows how to wind it down with Prince's sexy "Little Red Corvette."

1. "Welcome to the Jungle," Guns N' Roses
2. "Wanted Dead or Alive," Bon Jovi
3. "Flesh For Fantasy," Billy Idol
4. "You Give Love a Bad Name," Bon Jovi
5. "Invincible," Pat Benatar
6. "Bad Medicine," Bon Jovi
7. "Ziggy Stardust," David Bowie
8. "The Warrior," Scandal
9. "I Hate Myself for Loving You," Joan Jett
10. "Little Red Corvette," Prince
11. "Livin' on a Prayer," Bon Jovi (on a brave night)
12. "Dream On," Aerosmith
13. "Never Tear Us Apart," INXS
14. "Don't Cry," Guns N' Roses
15. "Blaze of Glory," Bon Jovi

DAVID, LOS ANGELES, CALIFORNIA

David knows how to shock with awesome lyrics. With lines like, "My pony, ride it, get on it," David's performances never fail to amuse, especially with his "pony" pelvis thrusts.

1. "Pony," Ginuwine
2. "Believe," Cher
3. "1, 2 Step," Ciara and Missy Elliott
4. "Wuthering Heights," Kate Bush
5. "All I Wanna Do Is Make Love to You," Heart (awesome lyrics)
6. "All Time High," Rita Coolidge

7. "Girls & Boys," Blur
8. "Miss Me Blind," Culture Club
9. "Lips Like Sugar," Echo & the Bunnymen
10. "Rocket Man," Elton John
11. "Mercedes Boy," Pebbles
12. "And She Was," Talking Heads
13. "Physical," Olivia Newton-John

ELISA, BROOKLYN, NEW YORK

Singable '90s classics are the songs that everyone will wish they had picked. Everyone knows "Love Shack" by the B-52's and "What's Up?" by 4 Non Blondes forward and backward. Plus, that one-hit wonder from the Proclaimers, "I'm Gonna Be (500 Miles)" is just plain infectious: "And I would walk 500 miles . . . na na na na . . ."

1. "Love Shack," The B-52's (it's best if a girl does Fred Schneider's part, in keeping with the Warholian gender-bending favored by the band)
2. "What's Up?," 4 Non Blondes
3. "Daydream Believer," The Monkees
4. "Yellow," Coldplay
5. "Creep," Radiohead
6. "I'm Gonna Be (500 Miles)," The Proclaimers
7. "Linger," The Cranberries
8. " Take on Me," a-ha
9. "Birdhouse in Your Soul," They Might Be Giants
10. "Stay (I Missed You)," Lisa Loeb

A veteran, Ben's choice of ballads, R&B classics, and new wave hits shows that his taste is anything but clichéd; he's an expert on more difficult songs that not everyone can sing along to.

1. "What You Won't Do for Love," Bobby Caldwell
2. "I Wanna Be Your Lover," Prince
3. "Shake You Down," Gregory Abbott
4. "Peg," Steely Dan
5. "Cracklin' Rosie," Neil Diamond
6. "Mack the Knife," Bobby Darin
7. "A Little Respect," Erasure
8. "Take on Me," a-ha
9. "Ignition," R. Kelly
10. "After the Love Has Gone," Earth, Wind & Fire
11. "Rip It Up," Orange Juice
12. "Precious and Few," Climax
13. "The Sun Ain't Gonna Shine Anymore," the Walker Brothers
14. "Eyes Without a Face," Billy Idol
15. "Always," Atlantic Starr (of course, you need to have a partner who knows the harmonies)

WHAT MAKES A GOOD KARAOKE SONG?

Not all great songs are great to sing. Remember, you *listen* to music; you *perform* (sing and dance to) karaoke. By the time you realize that "American Pie" is the most boring karaoke song ever, it'll be too late. Your crowd will have disbanded, having moved on to darts instead.

Karaoke is a social sport that depends on the exchange between the performer and the audience. You don't sing in a vacuum. So don't just sing for singing's sake. Pick a song for the people. You think to yourself, "'Say Say Say' is my favorite Michael Jackson and Paul McCartney collaboration. I like to sing it, therefore it *must* be good to karaoke." This is the number-one mistake of karaoke **newbs**: Just because you like it doesn't mean you should sing it.

FIVE CHARACTERISTICS OF A GOOD KARAOKE SONG

Like an outfit that looks good on the rack, you'll never know until you try it on. Following are five tips to help you sort the wheat from the chaff.

1. It's Easy to Sing

A good karaoke song shouldn't be too fast or, worse, too high. Fast songs are impractical since you won't be able to enunciate every word. Songs with too many high notes are worse—your voice might crack. A good karaoke song is accessible. It's a song you can sing with confidence. It'll make you look and sound great. Remember, *you* are on display, not just the music.

Too difficult: R.E.M.'s "It's the End of the World As We Know It" is too fast to flatter. We're not even sure it flatters Michael Stipe. Avoid "list songs," like "We Didn't Start the Fire" by Billy Joel.

Perfect: "I Want You to Want Me" by Cheap Trick. The vocal range is not too high or low, and most people can hit these notes. Though the lyrics are somewhat repetitive, it's good for people with short-term memory problems. And the melody is consistent throughout.

2. It's Short and Sweet

Karaoke is all vocals, so keep the instrumentals to a minimum. For example, "Africa" by Toto is a favorite of many, but it's almost entirely in one key, it's a whopping five minutes long, and it features a lot of instrumental downtime. Some songs have breaks that drag on and on. Others just have you repeat the last words of the chorus endlessly; "Total Eclipse of the Heart" by Bonnie Tyler comes to mind.

Bottom line—No karaoke song should be over four minutes (two and a half is ideal). People *will* get bored. For example, "Bohemian Rhapsody" should never be sung unless you have the operatic range of Freddie Mercury (which I'm betting you don't). Contrary to popular belief, it's not all about you. That's just **selfish karaoke.** You've got to make sure everyone else is having a good time, too.

Too long: "Sweet Transvestite" from the *Rocky Horror* soundtrack. It's a fantastic song that just happens to go on forever (five minuts).

Perfect: "Edelweiss" from *The Sound of Music*. It's short (just under two minutes), has few instrumental sections, and ends promptly.

3. Everyone Loves It

Sing something everyone loves. This is especially important at the beginning of the night. Woo the room with a universal hit. Guns N' Roses and Billy Joel are safe bets here.

Too obscure: The lesser-known Avril Lavigne songs. We don't even know what they are, so no one's going to pay attention when you sing them. Stick to the classics.

Perfect: "Summer Nights" from *Grease* or "Love Shack" by the B-52's. Both are easy-to-sing duets everyone knows. Even if you're not a great singer, people will be too busy singing along to care.

4. The Lyrics Stand Out

Get the crowd's attention by singing a song with a story ("All I Wanna Do Is Make Love to You" by Heart) or demands action ("Pour Some Sugar on Me" by Def Leppard). Dramatic lyrics can be matched with large-motion dancing and floor writhing.

Too muddled: "I Don't Want to Wait," Paula Cole.

Perfect: "Rock You Like a Hurricane," Scorpions.

5. It's Just Plain Good

What makes a "good song" is subjective. We're all guilty of liking bad music from our rosier, younger years; we all claim that *our* songs are the best. That's fine. Just know *your* songs well. But see if "The Sign" by Ace of Base sounds as good today as it did in '94. While some claim it's a classic, others will argue it's a flash in the pan. Test your selections—when a crowd gets excited for a song, you can bet it's a good one.

There are such things as perennial classics. These are songs that ripen with age—the jazz standards, Motown, oldies, Prince, Barbra Streisand, pre-1990s Billy Joel. A good song doesn't go out of style.

Too lame: "Barbie Girl" by Aqua has no repeat value. It's not even good in an ironic way. You might get excited to see it listed, but steer clear of songs that don't stand the test of time.

Perfect: "Old Time Rock and Roll" by Bob Seger. Everyone loves it. It's not monotonous and it has lyrics everyone knows. Songs by the Supremes, Elvis, or Jimmy Buffett are also gold.

SET LIST IS A SIGNATURE

A set list is your signature as a singer. It's a repertoire that is unabashedly you. A metalhead blasts power ballads, AC/DC, and a little Kenny Rogers at the end. A pop princess chooses Bacharach through Beyoncé. But whatever your mix is, own it.

When making your set list, stay away from played-out songs. It's fine to sprinkle your list with classics, but it's always better to resurrect forgotten favorites. One-hit wonders work well for this purpose because people usually can't remember the song or band name but will ultimately recognize the song. Night Ranger's "Sister Christian" and the Buggles' "Video Killed the Radio Star" are gems.

CREATE YOUR SET LIST

Draw up a list of at least thirty songs. Then start eliminating any that are unreasonably high-pitched (Mariah and Céline come to mind) or have monotonous lyrics (most songs by the Police). Check the variety: A mix of modern songs (from Jay-Z to The Killers) is great, but old standards tend to have more variation in vocal range. Songs like "Crazy" by Patsy Cline or anything from Ol' Blue Eyes make the grade.

If you're stumped, try one of these sources to help you compile your set list. Troll iTunes playlists online, your friends' playlists, and your parents' music collection. Google made-for-TV record compilations, like the *Oldies But Goodies* and *Best of the '80s* collections. Cherry-pick songs from your favorite movie soundtracks. Hang out at the record store. Tune in to the local easy-listening radio station (easy listening makes for easy singing). Or go no further than the lists compiled on pages 89–111.

TIP: BE ENCORE READY

Your set list should be between fifteen and twenty songs. Err on the side of excess—you never know what songs are available.

FINAL PRE-BAR PREP

Once you've made your set list, test-drive each song. How will you know if "Hollaback Girl" is truly amazing unless you've sung every last note? (Except for the "b-a-n-a-n-a-s" part, "Hollaback" is sort of boring to sing.) Start in the shower. On your daily commute. Sing for your parents, your best audience. Start practicing wherever with whomever. Actual mic practice is best with private karaoke setups: home systems or **karaoke box** private rooms (see page 39). If you can bear listening to your voice, tape-record yourself, play it back, and listen. Better you cringing than your audience.

Also think about trying different version of songs ("Killing Me Softly" by the Fugees vs. "Killing Me Softly" by Roberta Flack, for example). You may find older versions are slower and sometimes easier to sing ("Islands in the Stream" vs. "Ghetto Superstar"). Be wary of bastardized remakes such as Madonna's version of "Don't Cry for Me Argentina," which has a thumping house beat.

Remember: bring your set list and *Hit Me With Your Best Shot!* to karaoke. Always!

TIP: ROTATE YOUR TIRES

If you're about to wear the treads off your set list, it's time to rotate your tires. You've sung "Xanadu" so many times that you've practically been there on your roller skates. Keep it fresh; bring in the new. Go outside of your comfort zone. Experiment. If you're a show tunes kind of gal who lives for *Phantom*, try Joan Jett instead. If you're a metalhead, try some smooth R&B. Change keeps you from getting too comfy, which is good for experts and **newbs** alike.

THE SET LISTS: SONGS THAT MAKE THE WHOLE WORLD SING

Not a definitive catalog by any means, the following set lists culled by genre and occasion are here to inspire experimentation. Combine and remix. Make it awesome. Make it yours. **(Songs marked with * are duets.)**

GET THIS PARTY STARTED

We're all sheepish at the beginning; no one knows what to sing and no one wants to go first. Use these upbeat jams to kick-start the night. It'll get everyone toe-tapping, if not body-slapping.

"Faith," George Michael (or anything else by George Michael)

"What You Waiting For?," Gwen Stefani

"Tainted Love/Where Did Our Love Go?," Soft Cell

"Push It," Salt-N-Pepa

"Bette Davis Eyes," Kim Carnes

"Dancing With Myself," Billy Idol

"I Hate Myself for Loving You," Joan Jett

"Rock Your Body," Justin Timberlake

"Poison," Bell Biv DeVoe

"No Scrubs," TLC

"ABC," The Jackson Five

"Bye Bye Bye," 'N Sync

"Toxic," Britney Spears

"It's Not Unusual," Tom Jones

"Wake Me Up Before You Go-Go," Wham!

"I'm So Excited," Pointer Sisters

"I Think We're Alone Now," Tiffany

DUETS*

If you're new to karaoke, rely on strength in numbers. It's less daunting with a partner-in-crime who can carry half the vocals. Duets are great for serious performer types; a bigger cast means a bigger show. A dance or a routine (for "Summer Nights," for example) will turn karaoke into *Cabaret*.

"Let's Call the Whole Thing Off," Ella Fitzgerald and Louis Armstrong

"Summer Nights," Olivia Newton-John and John Travolta

"I Got You Babe," Sonny & Cher

"Ain't No Mountain High Enough," Marvin Gaye and Tammi Terrell

"Endless Love," Diana Ross and Lionel Richie

"Love Shack," B-52's

"Always," Atlantic Starr

"The Girl Is Mine," Michael Jackson and Paul McCartney

"Walk This Way," Run DMC and Aerosmith

"What Have I Done to Deserve This?," Pet Shop Boys featuring Dusty Springfield

"Feelin's," Loretta Lynn and Conway Twitty

"Don't You Want Me," Human League

"Islands in the Stream," Dolly Parton and Kenny Rogers

"Candy," Iggy Pop and Kate Pierson

"I'll Be There," Mariah Carey and Trey Lorenz

Their ubiquity doesn't mean you should pass them by. They're favorites for a reason. They're easy to sing. But remember, when singing the standards, yours needs to be over-the-top to stand out.

"Summer Nights," Olivia Newton-John and John Travolta*

"Margaritaville," Jimmy Buffett

"Feelings," Morris Albert

"More than Words," Extreme

"Crazy," Patsy Cline

"Love Shack," B-52's*

"Old Time Rock and Roll," Bob Seger

"Twist and Shout," The Beatles

"Don't Know Why," Norah Jones

"Friends in Low Places," Garth Brooks

"Paradise City," Guns N' Roses

"You Give Love a Bad Name," Bon Jovi

"Wind Beneath My Wings," Bette Midler

EASY-LISTENING BALLADS

It's the music you hear while in line at the drugstore—the soft-rock classics of yesteryear. Easy listening is one of the best genres for karaoke because the songs are easy to sing and are universally recognized. No one's willing to admit they love these slow jams, until you belt them out first.

"I Can't Go For That (No Can Do)," Hall & Oates

"Time After Time," Cyndi Lauper

"Landslide," Fleetwood Mac

"Goodbye Stranger," Supertramp

"Blue Bayou," Linda Ronstadt

"The Flame," Cheap Trick

"The Rose," Bette Midler

"Don't Dream It's Over," Crowded House

"Bette Davis Eyes," Kim Carnes

"Save a Prayer," Duran Duran

"Reminiscing," Little River Band

"Broken Wings," Mr. Mister

"Stay (I Missed You)," Lisa Loeb

"Dust in the Wind," Kansas

"Come Sail Away," Styx

MUSICALS

You don't have to be on 42nd Street to shine. Catchy and dramatic, these songs are for people who have always dreamed of being in musical theater. People love musicals more than they'd like to admit. Just get one started, and watch everyone else sing along.

"Xanadu," *Xanadu*

"My Favorite Things,"
   The Sound of Music

"Heart," *Damn Yankees*

"Sunrise, Sunset,"
   Fiddler on the Roof

"Sixteen Going on Seventeen,"
   The Sound of Music

"Some Enchanted Evening,"
   South Pacific

"On My Own," *Les Misérables*

"Don't Cry for Me Argentina," *Evita*

"Superstar," *Jesus Christ Superstar*

"What I Did for Love," *A Chorus Line*

"Tomorrow," *Annie*

"Tonight," *West Side Story*

"Summertime," *Porgy and Bess*

"Come What May," *Moulin Rouge*

"Seasons of Love," *Rent*

'60S GIRL-GROUP SONGS

Way before Destiny's Child, the Supremes, the Shirelles, and the Ronettes sang about the tribulations of the fairer sex. Great for karaoke, these classics are short, and they don't span the high and low notes.

"Stop! In the Name of Love,"
   The Supremes

"Be My Baby," The Ronettes

"It's My Party," Lesley Gore

"Baby Love," The Supremes

"The Loco-Motion," Little Eva

"My Boyfriend's Back," The Angels

"Baby It's You," The Shirelles

"Lipstick on Your Collar,"
   Connie Francis

"I Only Want to Be with You,"
   Dusty Springfield

"Downtown," Petula Clark

"Where Did Our Love Go,"
   The Supremes

YACH T ROCK

Inspired by the cult Internet show of the same name, Yacht Rock is the smooooothest soft-rock grooves of the '70s and early '80s. And the male leads won't kill your voice. So slip on your Top-Siders and croon like the most soulful white man around: Michael McDonald.

"I Keep Forgettin' (Every Time You're Near)," Michael McDonald

"This Is It," Kenny Loggins

"Love Will Keep Us Together," Captain & Tennille

"Rosanna," Toto

"Kiss on My List," Hall & Oates

"What a Fool Believes," The Doobie Brothers

"Sailing," Christopher Cross

"Summer Breeze," Seals & Crofts

"Hey Nineteen," Steely Dan

"Biggest Part of Me," Ambrosia

"I'm Not in Love," 10cc

"Watchin' the River Run," Loggins & Messina

SONGS FOR DISCO NIGHT

You don't have to wear polyester to hustle to these. But you will have to keep that booty moving; it would be just plain wrong to sing the Bee Gees standing still. With fast beats and long high notes, these disco anthems are for the well-trained singer. But you can work your way up to being a Super Trouper.

"Super Trouper," ABBA

"More Than a Woman," The Bee Gees

"You'll Never Find Another Love Like Mine," Lou Rawls

"Funkytown," Lipps Inc.

"Brick House," The Commodores

"I Will Survive," Gloria Gaynor

"Y.M.C.A.," Village People

"Super Freak," Rick James

"Love Is In the Air," John Paul Young

"Don't Stop 'Til You Get Enough," Michael Jackson

"Bad Girls," Donna Summer

"Dancing Queen," ABBA

"Don't Leave Me This Way," Thelma Houston

'80S TEEN MOVIES

Relive your prom and sing "If You Leave" at the end of your show. You'll get the crowd dewy-eyed remembering their first crushes. Most of these '80s songs are not hard to sing, but very dramatic. You'll invoke the memory of high-waisted jeans and Molly Ringwald.

"Somebody's Baby," *Fast Times at Ridgemont High*, Jackson Browne

"Pretty in Pink," *Pretty in Pink*, Psychedelic Furs

"Don't You (Forget About Me)," *The Breakfast Club*, Simple Minds

"Old Time Rock and Roll," *Risky Business*, Bob Seger

"Invincible," *The Legend of Billie Jean*, Pat Benatar

"Nothing's Gonna Stop Us Now," *Mannequin*, Starship*

"Glory of Love," *The Karate Kid Part II*, Peter Cetera

"In Your Eyes," *Say Anything. . .* Peter Gabriel

"Girls Just Want to Have Fun," *Girls Just Want to Have Fun*, Cyndi Lauper

"Hazy Shade of Winter," *Less Than Zero*, The Bangles

"If You Leave," *Pretty in Pink*, Orchestral Manoeuvres in the Dark

'80S NEW WAVE

The '80s were the first time in history when it was OK for straight men to wear neon and loads of eye makeup. With these songs, you'll have an excuse to put on your purple mascara and pegged pants again (even if you're male).

"Blue Monday," New Order

"Boys Don't Cry," The Cure

"Tainted Love/Where Did Our Love Go?," Soft Cell

"I Ran," A Flock of Seagulls

"Hold Me Now," Thompson Twins

"Voices Carry," 'Til Tuesday

"Flesh for Fantasy," Billy Idol

"Our House," Madness

"Obsession," Animotion

"Should I Stay or Should I Go?" The Clash

"The Metro," Berlin

"Sunday Girl," Blondie

"Owner of a Lonely Heart," Yes

"Hungry Like the Wolf," Duran Duran

"Take on Me," a-ha

"True," Spandau Ballet

"Let's Dance," David Bowie

GRUNGE

Dig out your plaid flannel shirts and tie 'em around your waist; it's time to rock Seattle all over again. Most of these songs are made up of guttural mumbling, so it won't matter if you can't get the words right. Just make them up.

"Evenflow," Pearl Jam

"Interstate Love Song," Stone Temple Pilots

"Disarm," Smashing Pumpkins

"Heart-Shaped Box," Nirvana

"Black Hole Sun," Soundgarden

"Runaway Train," Soul Asylum

"Man in the Box," Alice In Chains

"Plush," Stone Temple Pilots

"Shine," Collective Soul

"Smells Like Teen Spirit," Nirvana

"Everlong," Foo Fighters

'90S ALT KARAOKE

Karaoking these '90s alterna-songs seems so un-punk. But do it anyway, in honor of the ten-holed Docs in the back of your closet. Except for No Doubt, these are accessible to even the most vocally challenged. Blind Melon was already off-key, so anything you do will sound twice as good.

"Cannonball," Breeders

"Say It Ain't So," Weezer

"Cut Your Hair," Pavement

"Loser," Beck

"Big Time Sensuality," Bjork

"Sex and Candy," Marcy Playground

"Wonderwall," Oasis

"No Rain," Blind Melon

"Just a Girl," No Doubt

"Undone (The Sweater Song)," Weezer

"Closer," Nine Inch Nails

"Ironic," Alanis Morissette

"Longview," Green Day

THE KING OF POP

He's led a strange and interesting life, but you can't deny that MJ has style. And he was the first one to grab his crotch on stage (before Madonna). These songs are challenging and are best for higher, femmy voices.

"Ben"

"Thriller"

"Rock With You"

"Don't Stop 'Til You Get Enough"

"Billie Jean"

"Beat It"

"P.Y.T. (Pretty Young Thing)"

"Bad"

"Black or White"

"Say Say Say" with Paul McCartney*

"Human Nature"

"Man in the Mirror" (invoke irony here)

"The Way You Make Me Feel"

VINTAGE MADONNA

Before she started studying Kabbalah and modeling Versace, she was a dance-floor queen. Universal favorites, Madge's songs are easy for men and women of all vocal types to sing.

"Lucky Star"

"Borderline"

"Material Girl"

"Like a Virgin"

"Crazy for You"

"Burning Up"

"Like a Prayer"

"La Isla Bonita"

"Papa Don't Preach"

"Into the Groove"

"Holiday"

CLASSIC COUNTRY

Even city slickers can put on their cowboy hats for these classics. Ham it up with your best Western drawl. The best thing about country songs is that most everyone can sing 'em.

"Don't It Make My Brown Eyes
    Blue," Crystal Gayle
"Mammas Don't Let Your Babies
    Grow Up To Be Cowboys,"
    Waylon Jennings and
    Willie Nelson*
"Queen of Hearts," Juice Newton
"Ring of Fire," Johnny Cash
"On the Road Again,"
    Willie Nelson

"(I Never Promised You A) Rose
    Garden," Lynn Anderson
"The Gambler," Kenny Rogers
"I Walk the Line," Johnny Cash
"Rhinestone Cowboy,"
    Glen Campbell
"D-I-V-O-R-C-E," Tammy Wynette
"Crazy," Patsy Cline

KARAOKE-GRADE HIP HOP

No one expects the bar to have "C.R.E.A.M." by Wu-Tang, but there are some hip-hop classics found in most songbooks. Even if you sound more Betty Boop than B.I.G., try to pull these off with a straight face

"White Lines (Don't Do It),"
    Grandmaster Flash and
    Melle Mel
"Wild Thing," Tone Lōc
"Bust a Move," Young MC
"Supersonic," J.J. Fad
"Mr. Wendal," Arrested
    Development
"Killing Me Softly," The Fugees

"I Need Love," LL Cool J
"O.P.P.," Naughty By Nature
"Rump Shaker," Wreckx-N-Effect
"Baby Got Back," Sir Mix-A-Lot
"It Takes Two," Rob Base and
    DJ E-Z Rock
"Summertime," DJ Jazzy Jeff &
    The Fresh Prince*

ROCK YOU LIKE A HURRICANE

Rocking like a hurricane is about bringing the house down. It's about destroying everything in the way of your karaoke. These songs do just that. Not for the faint of heart, these full-powered anthems will inspire the layered-haired hesher in everyone.

"Welcome to the Jungle,"
    Guns N' Roses
"Rock You Like a Hurricane,"
    Scorpions
"We Are the Champions," Queen
"Wanted Dead or Alive," Bon Jovi
"Mony Mony," Billy Idol
"Take Me Out," Franz Ferdinand
"Heartbreaker," Pat Benatar
"Sweet Child O' Mine,"
    Guns N' Roses

"Legs," ZZ Top
"White Wedding," Billy Idol
"You Give Love a Bad Name,"
    Bon Jovi
"Walk This Way," Aerosmith and
    Run DMC*
"Poison," Alice Cooper
"Sister Christian," Night Ranger
"Crazy Crazy Nights," Kiss

HEADBANGERS

Like the above category, but more hardcore. Bring back the faded black band T-shirts and thrashing. And try not to break any air guitars onstage.

"I Love Rock 'N' Roll," Joan Jett & the Blackhearts
"You Shook Me All Night Long," AC/DC
"Iron Man," Black Sabbath
"Dr. Feelgood," Mötley Crüe
"Paradise City," Guns N' Roses

"Here I Go Again," Whitesnake
"Enter Sandman," Metallica
"Pour Some Sugar on Me," Def Leppard
"Cum On Feel the Noize," Quiet Riot

IT'S A MOD, MOD WORLD

If you're a mod (not a rocker), then these '60s, '80s, and '90s favorites will bring out the Anglophile in you. Vespas and Fred Perry attire are optional.

"Wonderwall," Oasis
"Girls & Boys," Blur
"Live Forever," Oasis
"You Really Got Me," The Kinks
"Time of the Season," The Zombies
"Daydream Believer," The Monkees
"Common People," Pulp
"Everyday Is Like Sunday," Morrissey (but you'll probably have to sing the 10,000 Maniacs version because they don't have this one at karaoke)

"Downtown," Petula Clark
"Always Something There to Remind Me," Naked Eyes
"Song 2," Blur
"Bitter Sweet Symphony," The Verve

JAMES BOND SONGS FOR SEDUCTION

The roguish spy has inspired ballads about jewels, one-night stands, and dying in the sexiest way possible. Use Bond songs to seduce your prey.

"All Time High," Rita Coolidge

"Goldfinger," Shirley Bassey

"Thunderball," Tom Jones

"A View to a Kill," Duran Duran

"For Your Eyes Only,"
    Sheena Easton

"Nobody Does It Better,"
    Carly Simon

"Diamonds Are Forever,"
    Shirley Bassey

"The Man with the Golden Gun,"
    Lulu

"You Only Live Twice,"
    Nancy Sinatra

SONGS WITH NUMBERS

You don't have to be good at math to sing about numbers. Try these as a pick-me-up when you're feeling down at tax time.

"2 Become 1," Spice Girls

"I'm Gonna Be (500 Miles),"
    The Proclaimers

"96 Tears," ? & the Mysterians

"867-5309/Jenny," Tommy Tutone

"1999," Prince

"18 and Life," Skid Row

"100% Pure Love," Crystal Waters

"1, 2 Step," Ciara and Missy Elliott*

"9 to 5," Dolly Parton

SAY MY NAME

Great people (and pets) have inspired some great songs. When serenading the object of your affection, try inserting his or her name into any one of these. But when singing "Ben" by Michael Jackson, don't tell your honey that the song is actually about Michael's pet rat.

"Sweet Caroline," Neil Diamond

"Oh! Carol," Neil Sedaka

"Ben," Michael Jackson

"Gloria," Laura Branigan

"Daniel," Elton John

"Sara Smile," Hall & Oates

"Rosanna," Toto

"Michelle," The Beatles

"Mickey," Toni Basil

"867-5309/Jenny," Tommy Tutone

SCI-FI AND FANTASY-THEMED SONGS

Geek is chic these days, so don't be afraid to sing these otherworldly tunes. Recommended for fans of *LOTR*, Renaissance Faires, D&D, and *The Legend of Zelda*.

"The Neverending Story," Limahl

"Mr. Roboto," Styx

"She Blinded Me With Science," Thomas Dolby

"Major Tom (Coming Home)," Peter Schilling

"Xanadu," Olivia Newton-John

"Self Control," Laura Branigan

"Eye in the Sky," The Alan Parsons Project

"Space Oddity," David Bowie

"Ziggy Stardust," David Bowie

"Together in Electric Dreams," Philip Oakey and Giorgio Moroder

"Video Killed the Radio Star," The Buggles

"99 Luftballons," Nena

"Sunglasses at Night," Corey Hart

"The Future's So Bright, I Gotta Wear Shades," Timbuk3

"Forever Young," Alphaville

DRIVING SONGS

Your car is one of the best places to sing: no complaints from neighbors and no crowds to please. With the volume turned way up, **car-aoke** is the ultimate pastime, whether you're stuck in gridlock or embarking on the Great American Road Trip.

"(Get Your Kicks On) Route 66," Nat King Cole

"Behind the Wheel," Depeche Mode

"Cars," Gary Numan

"Drive," The Cars

"I Drove All Night," Roy Orbison

"Drive My Car," The Beatles

"Freeway of Love," Aretha Franklin

"The Long and Winding Road," The Beatles

"Little Red Corvette," Prince

"Mustang Sally," Wilson Pickett

"Greased Lightnin'," John Travolta

"Get Outta My Dreams, Get Into My Car," Billy Ocean

WORKING FOR THE MAN

Working sucks. In the eternal words of Loverboy, everybody's working for the weekend. Rile up the nine-to-fivers when you sing these at happy hour.

"Everything She Wants," Wham!

"Morning Train (Nine to Five)," Sheena Easton

"(You Gotta) Fight for Your Right (To Party)," Beastie Boys

"She Works Hard for the Money," Donna Summer

"Lookout Weekend," Debbie Deb

"9 to 5," Dolly Parton

"Manic Monday," The Bangles

"Mo Money Mo Problems," The Notorious B.I.G.

"Working for the Weekend," Loverboy

MAKE 'EM CRY

Songs so heartfelt they make you want to curl up and cry. Sing with irony or with all your heart. Not recommended for the recently dumped.

"She's All I Ever Had," Ricky Martin

"Just Another Day," Jon Secada

"I Could Fall in Love," Selena

"Make It Real," The Jets

"Man in the Mirror,"
    Michael Jackson

"Love Me Tender," Elvis Presley

"To Be With You," Mr. Big

"(Everything I Do) I Do It for You,"
    Bryan Adams

"You're Beautiful," James Blunt

"Sometimes When We Touch,"
    Dan Hill

GAY OR EUROTRASH?

Put on your best British accent. You'll be mistaken for twee or trashy. It's a fine line; tread it!

"A Little Respect," Erasure

"Bizarre Love Triangle," New Order

"Regret," New Order

"Policy of Truth," Depeche Mode

"What's on Your Mind (Pure
    Energy)," Information Society

"Always on My Mind,"
    Pet Shop Boys

"The Promise," When in Rome

"Everything Counts,"
    Depeche Mode

"Living in Oblivion," Anything Box

"Pictures of You," The Cure

"Dreaming," Orchestral
    Manoeuvres in the Dark

"I'm Too Sexy," Right Said Fred

MIDDLE OF THE ROAD (MOR)

Do jangly, wimpy rock songs rock your sensitive soul? Then maybe you're into MOR. In ten years these might become ironic classics in the style of Peter Cetera. Until then, they are unbelievably MOR. Sing 'em for the ultimate ironic statement.

"Hey Jealousy," Gin Blossoms

"Mr. Jones," Counting Crows

"Run-Around," Blues Traveler

"Only Wanna Be with You,"
    Hootie and the Blowfish

"Breakfast at Tiffany's,"
    Deep Blue Something

"I'll Be There for You,"
    The Rembrandts

"Laid," James

"Satellite," Dave Matthews Band

"All I Want," Toad the Wet Sprocket

"3 A.M.," Matchbox Twenty

AIN'T THAT AMERICA

We are a proud people. We like to sing about ourselves. Just ask the Boss. U! S! A! U! S! A! Best after watching the Olympics, the World Cup, or any other international sports event.

"Born in the U.S.A.,"
    Bruce Springsteen

"Pink Houses," John Mellencamp

"Living in America," James Brown

"America," Neil Diamond

"America," *West Side Story*

"American Girl," Tom Petty

"Jack & Diane," John Mellencamp

"Young Americans," David Bowie

"American Woman," Lenny Kravitz

"Kids in America," Kim Wilde

NEW YORK VS. L.A.

New Yorkers have subways, seasons, and Billy Joel. Angelenos have endless summers, spacious homes, and Ice Cube. Sing out the rivalry with songs about the two greatest American cities.

NEW YORK

"New York State of Mind,"
Billy Joel

"New York, New York,"
Frank Sinatra

"Downtown Train," Tom Waits

"Tom's Diner," Suzanne Vega

"Arthur's Theme (Best That You
Can Do)," Christopher Cross

"Stayin' Alive," The Bee Gees

"Walk on the Wild Side," Lou Reed

L.A.

"All I Wanna Do," Sheryl Crow

"I Love L.A.," Randy Newman

"L.A. Woman," The Doors

"To Live and Die in L.A.,"
Wang Chung

"Welcome to the Jungle,"
Guns N' Roses

"California Love," 2Pac and Dr. Dre*

"California Dreamin'," The Mamas
and the Papas

"Nuthin' but a 'G' Thang," Dr. Dre
and Snoop Dogg*

O CANADA! SONGS BY CANADIANS

They look like us, rock out like us, live next door to us; the only difference is they're Canadian! They include Alanis, Avril, and Nelly Furtado. Here's a tribute to our neighbors to the north!

"Complicated," Avril Lavigne

"Maneater," Nelly Furtado

"Heaven," Bryan Adams

"Ironic," Alanis Morissette

"Summer of '69," Bryan Adams

"Sk8er Boi," Avril Lavigne

"I'm Like a Bird," Nelly Furtado

"My Heart Will Go On,"
   Céline Dion

"I Will Remember You,"
   Sarah McLachlan

"Hand in My Pocket,"
   Alanis Morissette

STRANGE LYRICS: TRY THEM IF YOU DARE

"99 Luftballons" is not about party favors. It's about nuclear fallout. And "Rapture" by Blondie is partially about a monster that'll eat your head. You won't realize how strange these songs are until you try them. Befuddle your audience.

"99 Luftballons," Nena

"Rapture," Blondie

"Rock Me Amadeus," Falco

"Bicycle Race," Queen

"Cornflake Girl," Tori Amos

"Mr. Roboto," Styx

"Calling Occupants of
   Interplanetary Craft,"
   The Carpenters

"Immigrant Song," Led Zeppelin

"Smooth Criminal,"
   Michael Jackson

I'M COMING OUT

You're totally gay. You haven't told your parents, so try coming out to them in a song. "It's a Sin" should do the trick, and if that doesn't work, "Y.M.C.A." Also perfect for your boys' night out.

"Finally," CeCe Peniston

"I'm Coming Out," Diana Ross

"Damn I Wish I Was Your Lover," Sophie B. Hawkins

"It's a Sin," Pet Shop Boys

"Come to My Window," Melissa Etheridge

"Heaven Is a Place on Earth," Belinda Carlisle

"Hand in Glove," The Smiths

"Live to Tell," Madonna

"Lola," The Kinks

"Believe," Cher

"Y.M.C.A.," Village People

"I Want to Break Free," Queen

INSPIRATIONAL WEDDING BALLADS

After many champagne toasts, serenade the couple of honor with these ballads. These songs simply say, "You're getting hitched," "It's the end of the line," and "Goodbye and good luck."

"We've Only Just Begun," The Carpenters

"We're All Alone," Rita Coolidge

"Unforgettable," Nat King Cole

"I Only Have Eyes for You," The Flamingos

"Always," Atlantic Starr*

"In My Life," The Beatles

"There's a Kind of Hush (All Over the World)," The Carpenters

"Happy Together," The Turtles

"Reunited," Peaches & Herb*

"We Belong," Pat Benatar

"Just the Way You Are," Billy Joel

"You're Still the One," Shania Twain

"I Don't Want to Miss a Thing," Aerosmith

YOUR CHEATIN' HEART

For cheats, temptresses, and cuckolds. Infidelity is just an unfortunate part of love, which is why it's the subject of so many songs. Lighten up, have a drink, and sing your woes.

"Secret Lovers," Atlantic Starr*

"Don't Cha," Pussycat Dolls

"Suspicious Minds," Elvis Presley

"Jessie's Girl," Rick Springfield

"Tempted," Squeeze

"It Wasn't Me," Shaggy

"Cry Me a River,"
    Justin Timberlake

"I Heard It Through the
    Grapevine," Marvin Gaye

"Lipstick on Your Collar,"
    Connie Francis

"Your Cheatin' Heart,"
    Hank Williams

"(If Loving You Is Wrong) I Don't
    Want to Be Right," Barbara
    Mandrell

SO IN LOVE

You're so in *love*. Doe-eyed euphoric love, and you just want to sing all the time. Try not to gross everyone else out—sing these to your honey behind closed doors.

"Beautiful," Snoop Dogg

"And I Love Her," The Beatles

"This Guy's in Love With You," Herb
    Alpert and the Tijuana Brass

"My Funny Valentine," Chet Baker

"I Only Want to Be With You,"
    Dusty Springfield

"Somebody," Depeche Mode

"Your Precious Love," Marvin Gaye
    and Tammi Terrell*

"I've Got You Under My Skin,"
    Frank Sinatra

"Masterpiece," Atlantic Starr

"Your Song," Elton John

"I Will Follow Him,"
    Little Peggy March

"Crazy for You," Madonna

"Close to You," The Carpenters

GIRLS' NIGHT OUT

Like *Sex and the City*, Manolo Blahniks, and Norah Jones, this set list is dude-proof. No boys will steal these girly jams. Can you say bachelorette party?

"Kiss Me," Sixpence None the Richer

"My Heart Will Go On," Céline Dion

"Don't Know Why," Norah Jones

"Breakout," Swing Out Sister

"Head to Toe," Lisa Lisa and Cult Jam

"Fallin'," Alicia Keys

"Hold On," En Vogue

"Whatta Man," Salt-N-Pepa

"Torn," Natalie Imbruglia

"Hit Me With Your Best Shot," Pat Benatar

"Real Love," Mary J. Blige

"Girls Just Want to Have Fun," Cyndi Lauper

"9 to 5," Dolly Parton

"Killing Me Softly," The Fugees

"Total Eclipse of the Heart," Bonnie Tyler

CAN'T STAND LOSING YOU

Love is a battlefield and you have the scars to prove it. Here are songs about how hard it is to let go. Best after a few cocktails and a tearful "she dumped me" session.

"Love Is a Battlefield," Pat Benatar

"Alison," Elvis Costello

"Nothing Compares 2 U,"
    Sinead O'Connor

"Don't Speak," No Doubt

"Don't Get Around Much
    Anymore," Harry Connick Jr.

"All Cried Out," Lisa Lisa and Cult Jam

"Sukiyaki," 4 P.M.

"You'll Never Find Another Love
    Like Mine," Lou Rawls

"Never Tear Us Apart," INXS

"All Around the World,"
    Lisa Stansfield

"I'll Never Fall in Love Again,"
    Dionne Warwick

"You Don't Have to Say You Love
    Me," Dusty Springfield

"The End of the World,"
    Skeeter Davis

"It's Too Late," Carole King

"You've Lost That Lovin' Feelin',"
    The Righteous Brothers

"Careless Whisper," Wham!

WHEN YOU'RE ON THE PROWL

With track names like "I Want Your Sex," this set list is self-explanatory.

"Doin' It," LL Cool J

"SexyBack," Justin Timberlake

"I Want Your Sex," George Michael

"In My House," Mary Jane Girls

"Rock With You," Michael Jackson

"I Want You to Want Me,"
    Cheap Trick

"Hungry Like the Wolf,"
    Duran Duran

"Oops (Oh My)," Tweet

"Naughty Girls (Need Love Too),"
    Samantha Fox

"Let Me Be the One," Exposé

"I'm Still in Love With You,"
    Al Green

"1, 2 Step," Ciara and Missy Elliott*

"Physical," Olivia Newton-John

"I Wanna Sex You Up,"
    Color Me Badd

AWESOME SONGS YOU SHOULD *NOT* KARAOKE (I'VE TRIED)

Too long, with too much bridge, or too-wack lyrics, these should not be attempted. Unless you are Bjork, don't try "All Is Full of Love." It's just wrong to butcher such a beautiful song.

"Africa," Toto

"Can't Get You Out of My Head,"
    Kylie Minogue

"Macarena," Los Del Rio

"American Pie," Don McLean

"Rapper's Delight,"
    The Sugarhill Gang

"Get Ready For This," 2 Unlimited

"The Final Countdown," Europe

"We Like to Party!," Vengaboys

"Gypsy Woman (She's Homeless),"
    Crystal Waters

"Pump Up the Jam," Technotronic

"All Is Full of Love," Bjork

"Don't Worry, Be Happy,"
    Bobby McFerrin

"Justified and Ancient," KLF
    featuring Tammy Wynette

"Return to Innocence," Enigma

"Hakuna Matata," Nathan Lane
    and Ernie Sabella

CHAPTER 7

KARAOKE TO GO-GO

At home. At the car wash. On the world-famous Internet. Karaoke doesn't have to be in the box or bar. In this chapter, you'll learn how to enable your iPod for that instant K-fix, find the best machine for home use, and get tips for growing your karaoke music collection. Best of all, discover all the Quirkyoke in the world. Pornaoke, anyone?

THE ULTIMATE KARAOKE DEN

You're out all hours gracing the mic. But your clothes smell like smoke and beer. You want to karaoke more hygienically. Somewhere closer. Say, your bedroom. So take it to the next level: Take karaoke home.

In a few steps, you can transform your home into a karaoke haven. Switch the tapestry curtains for purple velvet. Trade in the dining table for a bar. Dump the sconce for a disco ball. Optimize the layout for maximum acoustics. And of course, get all the gear. With some loungeworthy décor and a choice karaoke machine, you'll be able to entertain guests and, most important, your own fanatically singing self.

SINGING ACCESSORIES

To create the ultimate karaoke den, accessorize, accessorize, accessorize! Here are some basics.

Tambourine: Great for jangly songs like "Walk Like an Egyptian."

Triangle: Keep the musically challenged off the mic and hand them a triangle.

Cowbell: You can always use more cowbell.

Voice changer: Available at toy stores, voice changers let you sing anything in the style of Darth Vader.

Wigs: Everyone loves them, or loves to watch people make fools of themselves by wearing them.

Polaroid camera: Tack up a Hall of Fame/Shame behind the stage.

Songbook: Keep your song lists in plastic sheet covers in a three-ring binder. Keep two sections—one alphabetized by song and the other by artist.

Wet bar: Keep libations on hand. The kitchen counter, the wet bar (if you're lucky to actually have one), or the nightstand all provide great surfaces for your stock of adult beverages. Teetotalers need to wet their whistles, too, so don't forget the juice and tonic.

CHOOSE YOUR SYSTEM

Different systems serve different needs. Do you plan to entertain or sing for yourself? Do you need your system to be kid-proof and portable? Have you always dreamed of **car-aoke**?

Choosing a system can be daunting. Browsing karaoke sites, you'll see garish blinking ads, machines, and endless "greatest hits" collections. What's a **CDG** and do you have to buy all the weird peripherals? Will anything work with your Xbox? When you commit to a system, you'll amass a music library in one format, so choose wisely. The following is a comparison of formats by needs, price, and song quality.

FORMAT: COMPACT DISC + GRAPHICS (CDG)

SYSTEM: CDG players

BEST FOR: KJs, professionals, and singers who need the highest-quality songs for competitions.

THE LOWDOWN: CDGs are CD format but with graphics embedded in the disc. The discs can be played on any CD player, but the lyric graphics (a.k.a. **lyric teleprompter**) can only be accessed through a CDG player and a TV. A CDG player costs roughly the same as a DVD player ($100–200) and can be easily integrated into your home component system. You can also play the CDG format on a PC.

CDG is the format used by karaoke professionals (by KJs and at bars), since companies like **Sound Choice**, Music Maestro, and Blue Song make the most "faithful" versions. Hence, if you plan to sing on the bar circuit and are a stickler for a particular version of "The Rose" by Bette Midler, you should buy your own and ask the KJ to play your CDG when you're up. CDGs include roughly ten to twenty tracks and can be purchased individually. They range from $7–20.

When you buy "Popular Female Vocalists 8" for "Total Eclipse of the Heart," you also get stuck with a bunch of songs you'll never sing. Conveniently, a few publishers (**Sound Choice**, Music Maestro) offer custom CDG services, where you can order discs with only the songs you want (see "What To Buy, Where To Buy It," page 146).

THE VERDICT: Clunky, but mandatory if you plan to sing at competitions. Buy the authentic discs since most KJs refuse to play burned pirated copies. CDGs, however, will soon be phased out for digital formats, such as MPEG-4 (see below). Expect to hang on to a CDG player for two years, tops, before it becomes antiquated.

FORMAT: MPEG-4

SYSTEM: PC, iPod, doPi Karaoke

BEST FOR: Casual singers who don't want to buy peripheral karaoke equipment, and video iPod owners.

THE LOWDOWN: Companies that produce **CDG** music are making the same music available in a digital, downloadable MPEG-4 format, so expect the same high-quality versions of "My Heart Will Go On" as at the Karaoke Nationals. Like a CDG file, an MPEG-4 is an audio file embedded with graphical lyrics. But you won't need a CDG machine for playback—just a PC or a video iPod.

You can easily play MPEG-4 on PC media players like iTunes. But no one wants to party around a laptop. If you have a video iPod, you can karaoke on your home component system with a machine called doPi Karaoke ($50). DoPi, with the help of the video iPod, translates the video (lyrics graphics) to your TV. Plug your video iPod and mic into the doPi box, and sing off the TV.

THE VERDICT: If you want high-quality music from the biggest karaoke publishers for home karaoke, the digital MPEG-4 is the best format for you. It's cheaper and takes up less space than CDGs.

FORMAT: MIDI CARTRIDGES FOR MAGIC MICS

SYSTEM: All-in-one mics, Leadsinger, and **Magic Mic**
BEST FOR: Amateurs, part-timers, kids, and seniors.
THE LOWDOWN: Karaoke inside a single microphone? No way. Way! "Magic Mics" (as they're called in the Philippines) can be plugged into your TV via RCA cables, like a DVD player. Stateside, a company called Leadsinger distributes a similar product. The system comes with two mics (one wireless) and usually includes hundreds of preprogrammed songs. But the main mic also has expandable slots for song cartridges, and you can purchase additional cartridges by genre (country, Christian, Russian, or Tagalog, for example). A spiral-bound songbook is also included; additional cartridges come with inserts to expand your song collection.

The all-in-one is the best system for amateurs who aren't bothered by the tinny computer interpretations of Steve Miller Band (the songs do sound like they were composed on a Casio). Some Magic Mic songs sound better than others, but it's still not the format of choice for the **Karaoke World Championships** in Finland—**CDGs** are. But portable and incredibly idiot-/childproof, Magic Mics are probably the best bang for your buck. They're great for drunken guests, children, and grandparents who can't hear the difference. But don't practice for the Northwest Regionals on one.
THE VERDICT: Easy to use and hard to break, this is the workhorse of karaoke machines. It's the least expensive, too.

FORMAT: iKARAOKE

SYSTEM: iPod
BEST FOR: The casual singer who doesn't care about sound quality, and video iPod owners.
THE LOWDOWN: A mic for your iPod, the iKaraoke mutes the vocal on any non-karaoke music, thus turning any song into karaoke. But because it just uses any old music file, there's no **lyrics teleprompter** function. The device plugs into the charging slot of the iPod, which you then plug the headphones or a stereo output into. A switch on the side of the mic lets you go between vocals (original song) and non-vocals.
THE VERDICT: The vocal muting doesn't really work; it just reduces the sound quality to sound like a warped mono record. And because the mic cord is so short, you also won't be doing a floor slide when you're Tom Jones–ing. The iKaraoke is best relegated to sing-alongs in the car.

GROW YOUR MUSIC COLLECTION

Once you've picked the system, it's time to get music. Tons of sites and stores sell specialized karaoke equipment, and even major chain retailers like Best Buy carry karaoke machines, discs, and all-in-one cartridges. See the Resources section for more information.

AN UN-COMPACT DISC: THE LASER DISC

The laser disc went the same sad way of the cassette tape and the 8-track. These giant, LP-sized discs were made popular when they become the dominant format for karaoke in Asia and in Asian households. LD was the format for high-quality movies (and there was a decent selection back in 1990). But mainstream Americans did not have LD players, and if you had one, it was because your Asian parents were really into karaoke.

Made by Pioneer, the standard system (my parents owned two) had two mic inputs in the front of the deck, and a tray for LD loading. Just like a record, songs were recorded on both sides. When you were done with one side you had to eject and flip it. More advanced decks had "auto-reverse," saving you the trouble of getting off the couch. Produced in Asia, LD karaoke also offered low-budget karaoke videos (see "The Origin of Karaoke Videos," page 42).

The system, however, was clunky and expensive. The discs scratched easily and were expensive to replace. LD karaoke was phased out in favor of VCDs, DVDs, and, for professionals, **CDGs**. If you want a glimpse of the olden days, you can still catch LDs at Chinatown dive bars like Winnie's in New York City (see "Legendary Karaoke Spots," page 140). A KJ will have a stack of discs five feet high, and you can watch him change out those giant discs at every song.

WEB KARAOKE

The World Wide Web is just another forum for your impassioned Cher impression. So make a profile, plug in a USB mic, record, and upload. Get ratings and criticism *American Idol*–style, and excessive message board flattery by anyone and everyone. Online stardom is just a click away.

The three biggest sites—Bix, kSolo, and Singshot—all do basically the same thing: they supply the music, recording software, and social networking. The fourth site, Singer's Showcase, is for the karaoke professional (an oxymoron) who wants honest feedback. Here's a breakdown:

BIX.YAHOO.COM

PRICE: Free
VIDEO ENABLED: Yes
PLATFORM: PC only

Bix certainly has the most outlandish contests, such as the Best Yodel Contest, Sing for Your Servicemen Contest, and many that have nothing to do with singing—Favorite Pet Picture or Favorite Nintendo Character Contest. The interface is like other Yahoo services: cluttered, unattractive, and confusing. But it's also the only karaoke site that offers video content. That means instead of just listening to random strangers, you can see them crooning and wiggling at their computer stations. Take that as a pro or a con.

KSOLO.COM

PRICE: Free
VIDEO ENABLED: No
PLATFORM: PC only

With a similar library to Singshot.com (**Sound Choice** supplies the songs for both), kSolo.com has a quarter of the standards you'd want, but it's a decent online package. While they could do with more current titles, it's not a bad karaoke starter site.

SINGERSSHOWCASE.COM

PRICE: Free
VIDEO ENABLED: No
PLATFORM: PC and Mac

An offshoot of KaraokeScene.com, Singer's Showcase is for the careerist. It's a forum with constructive feedback and community. SS people even get together offline. There's also no irony or fooling around—SS comprises KJs and karaoke lifers.

SINGSHOT.COM

PRICE: Two-week membership, free; monthly fee, $9.95
VIDEO ENABLED: No
PLATFORM: PC and Mac

The best-looking of the bunch, Singshot is the most usable and accessible, being Mac- and PC-capable. Its Flash Player recording interface is easy to use, but it takes a while to sync your singing with the tempo of the song—it seems that the online playback is a little off. And although it's the best interface, it has a substantial monthly fee.

KARAOKE, THE VIDEO GAME

If you have a PS2 or Xbox and don't want to buy peripherals, getting a game is the easiest way to karaoke at home.

KARAOKE REVOLUTION

CONSOLE: PS2 and Xbox

PRICE: $50

Karaoke Revolution comes with a USB hands-free headpiece mic à la Janet Jackson in "Rhythm Nation." You select an avatar (big-haired rocker girl, Japanese pop star) and a song. When the song begins, the lyrics scroll at the bottom of the screen along with notes indicating high or low pitch. Follow the lines with your voice and change the pitch accordingly. However, the game can't measure if you are singing an exact middle G. You could be singing a middle B, and as long as you're holding it for the appropriate length of time, you will still get points. If you sing in an entirely different pitch than the real song, the game won't pick it up; it can only sense variations in pitch, not the pitch itself. The game offers a great selection of standards, and the expansion packs offer a few more songs.

KARAOKE REVOLUTION: AMERICAN IDOL

CONSOLE: PS2

PRICE: $54.99

If you don't have the luck or talent to get on **American Idol**, the next best thing is the game, which includes an excellent selection of *Idol* hits. Even better, caricatures of Paula, Simon, and Randy give you brutally honest advice. If you have the EyeToy camera, you can paste your picture onto a dancing Idol and be the star of your own karaoke video. This version of Karaoke Revolution also has a dance feature, à la Dance Dance Revolution. You can plug in your DDR floorpad (not included) and prepare to be doubly coordinated—dance and sing simultaneously.

QUIRKYOKE: UNCONVENTIONAL KARAOKE PRACTICES

In the backseat of a cab. Inside an ice-cream truck. In front of porn. Quirkyoke is a tribute to the strangest ways to sing.

THE BACKSEAT OF A CAB

The back of a taxi in Bangkok is not just a place to make out but a place to sing. Vichian Simma of Buriram installed a karaoke system in his cab. Charging the normal fare, this taxi is a musical ride above the rest. (Google "Vichian Simma" to learn more.)

INSIDE AN ICE-CREAM TRUCK

Karaoke Ice is a truck that cruises around San Jose offering free ice cream and karaoke to anybody off the street. A public installation created in conjunction with the San Jose Museum of Art, Karaoke Ice has tinny "ice-cream-truck music" renditions of "Material Girl" and "Don't Dream It's Over." It sounds like the Main Street Electrical Parade, but it's still karaoke. (Learn more at Karaokeice.com.)

AT THE CAR WASH

An older Filipino gentleman named Flo Apeles sells karaoke equipment and offers free singing at a West L.A. car wash while you wait. He says that he spent his whole life looking for that one passion in life until he found ". . . it was karaoke." Rinse, dry, sing, and repeat.

ALONG WITH PORNOGRAPHY

Pornaoke has nothing to do with singing. Pornaoke is "covering" moans and grunts from classic porn. The "singer" studies the porn sans sound and makes up a vocal track for the on-screen action. In San Francisco in the late '90s, the Odeon bar hosted pornaoke that was regular singing, only with porn playing on the video screen in the background. The end result, as newspapers noted at the time, was that even innocent songs could sound really really dirty, the Hokey Pokey probably being the best example: "You put your right hand in . . ." Like karaoke, pornaoke is about faking it. Takes place in the United Kingdom and various locations in the United States.

ON A MOBILE PHONE

If you can't get enough karaoke, here's a karaoke setup that you can keep in your pocket: mobile-phone karaoke. The music plays through phone speakers and the lyrics scroll on the tiny LCD screen. **Karaokini**, a Greek company, has achieved moderate success with their Java program. Other publishers such as **Sound Choice** have also created mobile karaoke software.

WITH A DICTIONARY

If you ever wanted to be serenaded by R2D2, it would sound like this. Dictionaraoke collects audio clips from online dictionaries pasted into pop songs of today and yesterday. (Learn more at Dictionaraoke.org.)

A GUIDE TO CAR-AOKE

Without a machine or a mic, singing is the natural thing to do when you're out on an open road . . . or a clogged interstate artery. The car is the best place to sing because no one can hear you. Even if they can, you'll never see them again. Remember, **car-aoke** is about transforming your entire vehicle into a moving speaker blasting YOU!

If you're a compulsive car singer, it has already occurred to you to car-aoke. It occurred to the Chinese—a Chinese automotive company called Geely is producing the first-ever car to include a built-in karaoke system. They know that it's one thing to just sing along to your favorite music, but it's another thing to hear your own sweet voice coming through the dash. So renew your license, get some insurance, and go cruising. God, think of all the driving songs you can sing (see "Driving Songs," page 102)!

Because of the iPod, most cars have input jacks for electronics, be it a PSP or a **Magic Mic.** But unless you have a headset mic, keep your hands at ten and two and watch your passengers have all the fun.

There are a few ways to set up car-aoke. Unfortunately, none of these include a way to use the **lyrics teleprompter**. But you should know all the words anyway.

- Plug portable systems like the Magic Mic into the input plug.
- Use iKaraoke (see page 118) with your iPod.
- Play a **CDG** (instrumentals) in your CD player and sing.

CHAPTER 8
THROW THE ULTIMATE KARAOKE PARTY

As Jay-Z promised, after the party, it's the afterparty. Built on the foundations of our idea of heaven—a choice song selection, ample singing opportunities, and a bottomless bar—home karaoke is an underrated social gold mine. Invite all your cute friends. With these melodic cocktail recipes, karaoke games, and other party tips, you'll be the hostess with the mostess.

PARTY STARTER

You're not throwing a mindless kegger. Karaoke gives the party a point: it's not one of those soirees where people just stand around looking too cool for school. Here's how to start it up.

1. DESIGNATE A KJ.

If you just let the music go on shuffle, there's the risk of dead air—a serious party faux pas. So designate a **KJ**/DJ for the night, hire a professional, or KJ yourself. No matter what, this person needs to be a serious music nerd, and a social regulator who knows how to rotate singers. He or she also needs an assertive hand to keep people in check.

2. SERVE FINGERLESS FOODS AND POWERFUL DRINKS.

This is a party where everyone will be touching the same mic and songbook, so it's a good idea to minimize the grease; fried finger foods are out. Keep toothpicks and mini forks handy for everything from fruit to pigs-in-a-blanket. Don't forget to stock your bar, too. Liquid courage is the perfect sauce for your main dish. And for the nondrinkers, get some sugary caffeine drinks.

3. INVITE PEOPLE WHO ARE REALLY GOOD AT KARAOKE.

Go out of your way to invite the really good singers, like the Professional (see "The Archetypes," page 45). He'll give people something to aspire to, and you'll get props for knowing the guy with *the voice*. And that girl who made it to the local karaoke championships, invite her too. She might not sing that well but she does know how to rile up a crowd.

4. PLAY AN INSPIRATIONAL MIX TAPE.

As people filter in, play your super-mix to get the crowd hyped. Choose cheerful standards like "Fly Me to the Moon," "I Love Rock 'N' Roll" by Joan Jett, "Stand by Your Man" by Patsy Cline, and anything by the Ramones. Remind everyone how much they loved Rita Coolidge, and that "All Time High" is a very moving karaoke song. They won't have **song block**—not knowing what song to pick—after your bumping mix.

5. KEEP *HIT ME WITH YOUR BEST SHOT!* HANDY.

It will inspire unbridled karaoke passion, especially the sample set lists at the end of Chapter 6. Your guests will get ideas for every foreseeable occasion and genre, like songs the brokenhearted should belt, or what's recommended for first-timers.

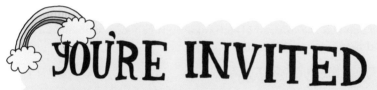

YOU'RE INVITED

YOU ARE CORDIALLY INVITED TO MY KARAOKE-A-THON, WHERE WE'RE GOING TO SING, TIL OUR VOCAL CHORDS BLEED FROM THE INSIDE.

✳TIME   **YOUR PRESENCE IS REQUESTED AT 8:30 P.M. AT 27 ORCHARD STREET.**

✳ DRESS   **PLEASE DRESS IN THE STYLE OF THE SINGER OF YOUR FAVORITE KARAOKE SONG. IF YOU LOVE "TOTAL ECLIPSE OF THE HEART," WE EXPECT YOU TO BE A SPITTING IMAGE OF BONNIE TYLER.**

✳BRING   **YOUR WELL-MANNERED, MUSIC-LOVING FRIENDS.**

✳ DON'T BRING   **ANYONE YOU WOULD NOT LEAVE UNATTENDED ON THE MIC OR IN YOUR OWN HOME.**

CROONING COCKTAILS

"The whole world is drunk and we're just the cocktail of the moment. Someday soon, the world will wake up, down two aspirin with a glass of tomato juice, and wonder what the hell all the fuss was about." —Dean Martin in *The Rat Pack*

A few fiery drinks in the belly will cease any civilized conversation and inspire you to hijack the mic. Try these custom cocktails by the Liquid Muse, my favorite mixologist. After your second drink you won't be able to handle anything too complicated, like putting your clothes back on. These drinks *will* achieve the desired effect: minimum self-consciousness and maximum vocal output.

SING-ALONG SLING

- 2 ounces of rum
- 1/2 ounce of blood orange bitters
- 3 ounces of pineapple juice
- Squeeze of lime
- Ginger beer

Shake the rum, bitters, and pineapple and lime juices with ice. Pour into an ice-filled Collins glass. Top with ginger beer. Goes best with "Sweet Home Alabama," "Tainted Love," or any other song that inspires messy group singing.

CLASSIC CROONER

- 3 ounces of Remy cognac
- Cointreau or Grand Marnier

Pour the cognac into a snifter and float the cointreau. Garnish with an orange peel swirl, if desired. Goes best with the classics, like Rat Pack or James Bond songs.

POP PRINCESS

- Squeeze of lemon
- $1/2$ ounce of raspberry liqueur
- Pink champagne
- Maraschino cherry

Pour the liquid ingredients into a chilled Champagne flute. Drop the maraschino cherry into the bottom of the drink. Input Britney, Tiffany, vintage Madonna, or any other pop-tart hit.

SCREECHING BANSHEE

- $1 1/2$ ounces of vodka
- 1 ounce of white chocolate liqueur
- 1 ounce of crème de banane
- 1 ounce of cream (or milk)

Shake the above ingredients well, with ice. Strain into a chilled, sugar-rimmed martini glass. Goes with classic metal. "Sister Christian" by Night Ranger most recommended.

Cocktail recipes courtesy of cocktail enthusiast Natalie Bovis-Nelsen (a.k.a. The Liquid Muse). Get inspired with more recipes and worldly cocktail trends on her blog: www.TheLiquidMuse.com.

KJ Tips

A **KJ** is the behind-the-scenes force that keeps the party moving forward. If you don't hire a professional, here are some tips for doing it yourself.

Have a Sign-Up Sheet
To keep brawls to a minimum, have a sign-up sheet attached to a clipboard. Include columns for the singer's name, song title, and song number. Keep it near the KJ booth and let the KJ be the arbiter of song order.

Rotate Singers
Even if Chatty Cathy put in the last five songs, it doesn't mean you have to play them. Rotate in Jeff, Patty, and John even if they are farther down on the list. Just because one person is quick to sign up doesn't mean she should sing five in a row. And if you don't rotate, your guests will get bored of Cathy and leave.

Step Up to the Mic
The KJ should have a mic to page the next singer and chat up the crowd when waiting for the next performer. Take a guess on the breakout act of the night, share a bit of trivia, or just make a comment about the last singer's gold lamé shoes. The KJ's duty is to entertain and inform.

Rotate Out the KJ
After two hours, any KJ will feel all played out. So keep a spare to relieve KJ number one. A KJ needs time to breathe, reflect, and down a whiskey before going back to the mic.

Play Games
Hard to believe, but some people need an incentive to sing. Games are a great way to involve non-singers. They help level the playing field, unnerving the best and worst equally.

PARTY GAMES

If you're just starting out, or if the night is going slowly, try a round of Karaoke Bingo or Fade Out Fade In. For folks with ADD, try Kamikaze. It's such a spectacle that it'll lure those hiding behind the snack bar to the mic. It'll also inspire a healthy competitive streak among the guests.

TIP: LEAD SINGER

To get any game started, the **KJ** or host may want to demonstrate each activity first.

KAMIKAZE

Also known as Russian Roulette, Suicide, and even Scaryoke, Kamikaze Karaoke is simple: you pick a random song out of a hat and perform it. It keeps everyone on their toes, because who can really prepare for Missy Elliott? It's fun to watch people triumph as well as crash and burn.

1. Depending on the number of players, write down the titles of fifteen to twenty songs on separate pieces of paper. Songs should vary in genre, artist, and decade, just to mix it up. If you have a crowd of **newbs,** don't choose difficult or obscure songs.

2. Fold each piece of paper and put in jar #1.

3. Ask each guest to write his or her name on a piece of paper, and then put into jar #2.

4. Shake both jars. Have the KJ draw a name from jar #2. Call up the singer. Then have the player draw a song out of jar #1.

5. The singer must perform the selected song!

AIR GUITAR ROCK-OFF

Make love to the air guitar, just like you did when you were a melancholy teen playing Zeppelin in your bedroom. For Slash wannabes, the Air Guitar Rock-Off will settle the question of who handles that imaginary Stratocaster best. Preparations are necessary, like a homemade cardboard guitar, since you probably want to keep your real Les Paul locked away from drunken partygoers. Remember, it's still karaoke, so everyone has to sing also.

1. Write up a sample **set list** of fifteen or more guitar-centric songs. Examples:
   a) "I Love Rock 'n' Roll," Joan Jett
   b) "Paradise City," Guns N' Roses
   c) "More Than a Feeling," Boston
   d) "Pour Some Sugar on Me," Def Leppard
   e) Anything by Jimi Hendrix
   f) "Piece of My Heart," Janis Joplin
   g) "Immigrant Song," Led Zeppelin
   h) "The Final Countdown," Europe
   i) "Livin' on a Prayer," Bon Jovi
   j) "Higher Ground," Red Hot Chili Peppers

2. Create a sign-up sheet with two columns: one for names and another for song titles.

3. Pass around both sheets so everyone can sign up for their favorite guitar jam.

4. Tell people that the cardboard guitar is optional, but encouraged.

5. Decide the winner: pass around small tabs of paper and have people fill in their favorite performance. Tabulate the results, and invite the winner for an encore.

KARAOKE BINGO

Karaoke Bingo works best if you have an awesome prize, and especially if your attendes have a decent attention span. Instead of numbers and letters, fill in genres, artists, and song titles. Make a different card for each player. A sample card looks like this:

R&B	CYNDI LAUPER	COUNTRY	"CRAZY"	BILLY JOEL
LOVE	ROCK	HEART	BEYONCE	MARY J. BLIGE
"ROCKET MAN"	"MORE THAN WORDS"	FREE SPACE!	KISS	MOTOWN
PAT BENATAR	THE SMITHS	"SUMMER NIGHTS"	THE BEATLES	"LOVE SHACK"
RAP	KELLY CLARKSON	"JUST LIKE HEAVEN"	BOB SEGER	POP

1. Distribute a bingo card and a pen to each player.
2. Each time one of these squares (genres, songs, or artists) is performed, players mark the spot. For example, if someone sings "True Colors," you can X off Cyndi Lauper.
3. You cannot mark two squares in one turn. For example, if someone sings Bob Seger, you can only mark off either "Bob Seger" OR the genre "Rock."
4. The first person with a line of five (across, down, or diagonal) who yells "Bingo!" wins.
5. You can also sing songs that will help you complete your card. For example, if all you need is a Kelly Clarkson song for the win, you can go sing it yourself.

To make a good bingo grid, gauge your crowd. Don't fill it to the brim with Travis Tritt if the crowd is strictly slow jams. Conversely, mix it up to push people out of their comfort zones. If all it takes to win is Mary J. Blige, then even Nick the metalhead will take a shot at "Real Love."

FADE OUT FADE IN

You know it so well you don't even need the music. Or do you? Fade Out Fade In tests how well you really know the song. Can you sing it **a cappella**?

1. The **KJ** picks a song for a contestant.

2. At an arbitrary point, the KJ fades out the song for fifteen to thirty seconds. When he fades the music back in, everyone will see if the singer is on or totally off.

3. Cast your votes for whomever is most on track.

RELAY

Can you and your BFF finish each other's sentences? Is she the Brandy to your Monica in "The Boy Is Mine"? Dubbed the Beastie Boy Syndrome, Relay is when two singers go back and forth, alternating lyrics. It goes like this:

1. Two people choose a song they know (or think they know) well.

2. They alternate lines like this:

    S1: Since you been gone
    S2: I can breathe for the first time
    S1: I'm so moving on yeah, yeah
    S2: Thanks to you
    S1: I can get
    S2: What I want
    S1: Since you been gone . . .

3. The duo who pulls this off the best wins.

THE CHAIN GAME

The Chain Game tests how well you can come up with song titles on the fly.

1. The **KJ** picks a favorite song ("Magic Carpet Ride") and sings it.

2. Singer #1 must then name a song with at least one of the same words as the KJ's song. For example, if the KJ picks "Magic Carpet Ride," Singer #1 can pick "Magic Man."

3. Singer #2 must then name a song with either Magic or Man in the title, such as "Man in the Mirror." Singer #3 can choose "I'll Be Your Mirror," and so on.

4. Anyone who blanks out on a song title, doesn't sing at all, or can't finish the song is out.

RESOUR
THE LIN

ES:

R NOTES

LEGENDARY KARAOKE SPOTS

The best karaoke isn't in gilded halls or even in the most metropolitan of cities; it happens anywhere. Here are reviews of some of the best.

DIMPLES
When: Nightly
Where: Burbank, California
Supposedly America's first karaoke bar, Dimples is a classic lounge near all the studios, so there are often wrap parties and celeb sightings. They make you go on stage in costume, wig and all, and then project your image on the outside of the building for all the passing cars to see. An institution.

BOARDWALK 11
When: Nightly
Where: Los Angeles, California
When you want to get away from the dives, Boardwalk 11 is a cross between a swank supper club and a locals' hangout. It draws everyone from sorority girls to octogenarians singing "Rump Shaker." One of L.A.'s finest, it has an excellent song selection and a relaxed vibe.

BRASS MONKEY
When: Nightly
Where: Los Angeles, California
Celebs (like Gwyneth Paltrow) and wannabes rush the stage at this Koreatown staple, which is the most well-known karaoke bar in town among the young professional set. But the Monkey gets very crowded nightly, so get there early if you plan to actually sing.

BOW BOW COCKTAIL LOUNGE
When: Nightly
Where: San Francisco, California
"Chinatown Dive" should be a category of classic karaoke bar, and Bow Bow is certainly the best of this group. Older Chinese folks, hipsters, and locals make this place a real neighborhood hang-out. Leave it to the hostess, aptly named Candy, to take care of you with good humor and the occasional on-the-house drinks.

7 BAMBOO
When: Nightly, except Monday and Sunday (closed)
Where: San Jose, California
This technologically advanced dive bar is an S.J. favorite. Everything is digitized, including inputting the song into a computer terminal. And you don't even have to be there to enjoy the singing—the computer-geek (and very human) **KJ** streams the performances live online. Expect a mixed crowd and plenty of support.

ARMIDA'S
When: Nightly
Where: Denver, Colorado
Authentic Mexican food, slightly cheesy décor, and karaoke seven nights a week (starting as early as 6:30!), Armida's is the spot for Denver karaoke. With a diverse crowd, from hipsters to nine-to-fivers, go on weekdays to avoid the rush.

CONTINUED...

MARY'S

When: Tuesdays, Saturdays
Where: Atlanta, Georgia
Down your Marytini, Something About Mary, or a Virgin Mary cocktail at this '50s-style throwback before you get on the mic. Karaoke is so popular at this eclectic neighborhood favorite that it's twice a week. Unlike at sports bars, here you're encouraged to belt Streisand, Neil Diamond, and Cher. There's no such thing as too much camp at Mary's.

THE PURPLE SHAMROCK

When: Tuesdays
Where: Boston, Massachusetts
Sweaty and crawling with college co-eds, the Shamrock is the kind of place where you don't want to wear good clothes, but can be sure that everyone is having a good time. Not a strict karaoke bar, but a good mix of dinner, dancing, and rollicking mischief; go to the Sham Tuesday nights to sing in front of a revved-up audience.

DUFFY'S TAVERN

When: Thursdays
Where: Lincoln, Nebraska
Duffy's blows up on Thursdays with live-band karaoke featuring local phenomenon Shithook. Playing classic and punk rock standards like Led Zeppelin, Violent Femmes, and AC/DC for over ten years, Shithook karaoke has garnered a cult following and become a Lincoln institution. No cover charge!

DJ'S DUGOUT

When: Nightly
Where: Omaha, Nebraska
A popular sports bar, DJ's is also the place to see pianists

duke it out in Omaha's only "dueling" piano bar. The catch is you have to get up and sing with them. They take requests, make up requests, and make up songs. Bonus: guest appearances by nationally known piano players.

THE IMPERIAL PALACE
When: Nightly
Where: Las Vegas, Nevada
Like Céline Dion and Wayne Newton, you too can be a real Vegas lounge act at the Imperial Palace, one of the liveliest karaoke venues in a city with more than two hundred. You can see locals, tourists, and real musicians perform in this historic landmark.

PUNK ROCK KARAOKE AT ARLENE'S GROCERY
When: Mondays
Where: New York, New York
PRK is hard rock hesher karaoke with a live band. You sign up and do your best Axl Rose for a packed house. PRK really does make you feel like a rock star. But like any real band karaoke, you better be able to deliver. Most people who perform are Lower East Side musicians who are already too good. It's sort of unfair.

SING SING
When: Nightly
Where: New York, New York
With its amazing song selection and ultra-polished floors, Sing Sing is a bar with private room rentals (call ahead for reservations). Private rooms also offer room service for drinks. The bar section is in a narrow long room where, if you're lucky enough to get a seat at the bar, you can sit while you sing. The main room gets overrun with college students later in the night.

CONTINUED...

WINNIE'S

When: Nightly
Where: New York, New York
One of the best dives in Chinatown, their song selection sucks, songs actually cost a dollar, and the mixed drinks are watered down, but the intimate dance floor, charming old-fashioned booths, and cheerful mixed crowd make up for it.

HIP-HOP KARAOKE AT THE KNITTING FACTORY

When: Monthly
Where: New York, New York
For those who feel traditional karaoke doesn't offer enough hip-hop, Hip-Hop Karaoke lets wannabe MCs duke it out every month at the Knitting Factory. There's no teleprompter, so you better know the words or this rough crowd will get bored. Usually turns into group rap-along, with too many MCs and not enough mics.

COLIN, THE KING OF KARAOKE

When: Tuesdays, Thursdays, Sundays
Where: various venues, New York City and Brooklyn, NY
The self-proclaimed king who KJ's with his amply packed laptop, Colin's boisterous singing parties are the stuff of New York legend. Carrying songs from Fugazi through New Edition, he's at Spunik (Brooklyn) on Tuesday, Alligator Lounge (Brooklyn) on Thursday, and Lit (Manhattan) on Sunday. But come prepared—Colin's cult following includes all the cool kids from local bands.

LIPSTICK LOUNGE

When: Tuesdays, Wednesdays, Thursdays
Where: Nashville, Tennessee
All are welcome to this laid-back Nashville gem that offers live band music, poker, trivia night, and, of course, karaoke for

a mixed gay and straight crowd. With a giant song library and cash competitions, Lipstick fills up fast, so get there early.

LONNIE'S WESTERN ROOM
When: Nightly
Where: Nashville, Tennessee
With memorabilia filling the walls, Lonnie's is a shrine to the country masters of Nashville's glorious past. The best karaoke in town, the place gets packed with a fun crowd. Though his joint is wildly popular and famous, Lonnie himself will still come out to bid you good night.

SPOTLIGHT KARAOKE
When: Nightly
Where: Houston, Texas
An Asian-style karaoke bar and private-room venue, Spotlight has an excellent song selection (Asian-language and English) and can be rented by the hour.

BEACON'S PUB
When: Fridays
Where: Seattle, Washington
With big songbooks and a diverse crowd (from sleazy to chichi), the Beacon is the quintessential dive-bar karaoke. A supportive crowd and friendly staff always keep the party going.

CLUB DIRECTORY
Don't live near any of the previous legendary bars? Then try this:

The Karaoke Scene Club Directory
www.karaokescene.com/directory
Karaoke Scene's directory tracks karaoke around the country by day and time.

WHAT TO BUY, WHERE TO BUY IT

MUSIC MANUFACTURERS

If you've just about worn out your *Oldies But Goodies* laser disc, it's time to go shopping. The following karaoke music publishers should be able to hook you up with some new tracks:

CHARTBUSTER
www.chartbusterkaraoke.com
KARAOKEMAKER (CANADA)
www.karaokemaker.com
LEADSINGER
www.leadsinger.com
MUSIC MAESTRO
www.musicmaestro.com
SINGKING (CANADA)
www.singking.ca
SOUND CHOICE
www.soundchoice.com
SUNFLY (UK)
www.sunflykaraoke.com
ZOOM (UK)
www.zoom-entertainments.co.uk

RETAILERS

No matter where you live, good karaoke supplies can be yours. The following online and on-site retail stores carry a wide assortment of music and equipment (machines, mics, sound systems).

ACE KARAOKE
www.acekaraoke.com
D.T.S. KARAOKE
www.dtskaraoke.com

KARAOKE.COM
www.karaoke.com
GOOD TIME KARAOKE
www.goodtimekaraoke.com

ALL TOGETHER NOW: THE KARAOKE COMMUNITY

There aren't any mainstream publications about the karaoke scene, but you can find karaoke news if you know where to look. Your best bet is looking locally, wherever you live, for the weeklies listing karaoke-related events. Meetup.com is also an excellent resource for meeting other local karaokers.

FORUMS, NEWS, AND PUBLICATIONS

The sites below are tight-knit communities filled with very knowledgeable K-heads. They'll let you in on new products, reviews, and professional KJ advice.

THE KARAOKE SCENE FORUM
www.karaoke-forum.com
It's the hangout for serious performers and professional KJs. A great place to get KJ advice on equipment issues. However, this forum is closely monitored and guarded, so be on your best behavior.

KARAOKE SCENE
www.karaokescene.com
An excellent resource for all things karaoke, the online version of *Karaoke Scene Magazine*.

NORTHWEST KARAOKE GUIDE

www.nwkaraokeguide.net
Chronicling the hotbed of karaoke, the Pacific Northwest, *The Northwest Karaoke Guide* has articles for enthusiasts and people just starting out.

THAT'S KARAOKE RADIO SHOW

www.thatskaraoke.com
That's Karaoke is a professionally-produced radio show featuring news for KJs and fans about the industry, new technologies, and the scene, and interviews with singers, KJs, and industry experts.

PLACES TO SING, CONNECT, AND COMMENT ONLINE

Who says you have to be out and about? Upload your performance and be judged accordingly. You're only a few clicks away from "Karaoke Idol."

BIX

www.bix.yahoo.com

KSOLO

www.ksolo.com

RONAN'S ONLINE KARAOKE

www.ronansonlinekaraoke.com

SINGSHOT

www.singshot.com

THE SINGER'S SHOWCASE

www.singersshowcase.com

SINGINGPHENOM

www.singingphenom.com

GLOSSARY

A cappella: Singing without musical accompaniment. Can be harmonized.

American Idol: A television talent search for America's next rock star, *Idol* is an elaborate karaoke contest where the grand prize is a recording contract, not just a microphone-shaped trophy and a free round of drinks at the pub.

Band-aoke: When a live band supplies the music for a karaoke vocalist.

Beermuffs: When judgment has been impaired by alcohol, Beermuffs is the phenomenon of thinking you sing and dance better than you actually do.

Cantopop: Cantonese pop music originating from Hong Kong. Popular artists include Faye Wong and Jacky Cheung. A popular genre to karaoke worldwide.

Car-aoke: Karaoke performed in the car.

CDG: Stands for Compact Disc + Graphics; the most popular format for KJs and competitive karaokers.

Entertainment value: A criteria of judging karaoke, includes the audience and judge's reaction to the overall performance.

Gian: Derived from the name of a character in the Japanese cartoon *Doraemon*, Gian refers to someone who loves to karaoke but sings horribly out of tune. Pronounced *ghee-on*.

Group karaoke: A messy group sing-along that occurs at the end of the night, usually with intoxication.

Juhachiban: Number eighteen in Japanese, *juhachiban* means the one song you are especially good at singing. *Juchiban* refers to the eighteen most popular Kabuki plays. Pronounced *ju-ha-chi-bon*.

Karaoke (*verb*): To karaoke is the act of singing live to prerecorded music. **Karaoking, karaoked** (p.t.).

Karaoker (*noun*): One who karaokes**.**

Karaoke box: Private rooms with individual karaoke system rented by the hour. *See also* **KTV.**

Karaoke World Championships: The worldwide karaoke competition held yearly in Finland. www.kwc.fi

Karaokini: A brand of mobile-phone karaoke produced in Greece. Karaokini is a downloadable application that allows phone users to read lyrics off the LCD phone screen.

KJ or Karaoke Jockey: Like a DJ, the KJ is the person who controls music at a karaoke bar or party.

KTV (Karaoke Television): The Chinese name for private room karaoke.

Lyrics teleprompter: A monitor display that features song lyrics in sync with the music.

Magic Mic: A karaoke microphone that has embedded songs and requires a monitor to display lyrics.

Mic hog: A song whore who monopolizes the mic.

Newb/Newbie: A neophyte, a singing frosh.

Noraebang: Korean for karaoke box. Pronounced *nor-ray-bon*. *See also* **karaoke box**.

Rhythm and tempo: The speed of the voice in relation to the music.

Rock Star Effect: The effect of good karaoke getting you dates and booty calls.

Selfish Karaoke: Singing songs no one else derives pleasure from listening to.

Set list: A list of personal best songs you sing particularly well.

Sing K: In Hong Kong, Sing K is slang for "going to a karaoke box."

Song block: A phenomenon that involves temporarily not being able to choose a song to sing, due to lack of inspiration or forgetting your set list at home.

Sound Choice: The largest karaoke music publisher in the United States.

Stage presence: How you carry yourself in your performance or the visual aspect. It can include charisma, improvisation, charm, and audience interaction.

Utagoe kissa: "Singing cafés" in Tokyo in the 1960s, where the audience sang in unison with live band music. A predecessor to karaoke.

Videoke: Karaoke music that features Asian-produced accompanying videos.

Vocal expression: How well the performer is able to express the meaning and mood of the song.

Voice and sound quality: The quality and uniqueness of a voice.

You've made it this far. Time to test your karaoke smarts. How much do you really know?

1. The first karaoke bar in America was
   a) Dimples in Burbank
   b) the Brass Monkey in Los Angeles
   c) the Imperial Palace in Las Vegas
   d) Winnie's in New York

2. Next to Japan, the largest karaoke market in the world is
   a) England
   b) the United States
   c) Finland
   d) Italy

3. The person who plays karaoke music at a bar is called
   a) a DJ
   b) a KJ
   c) a karaoke MC
   d) a KTV

4. In a scene-stealing performance, Cameron Diaz gave a tone-deaf rendition of _____ in *My Best Friend's Wedding*.
   a) "I Say a Little Prayer"
   b) "I Just Don't Know What to Do With Myself"
   c) "Be My Baby"
   d) "Crazy"

5. _____ hates karaoke.
   a) Tom Cruise
   b) Rachael Ray
   c) Amy Tan
   d) Jay Leno

6. TRUE or FALSE. Sex Pistols mastermind and media agitator Malcolm McLaren once wrote a manifesto on "Karaoke Culture."

7. _____ is too long for karaoke, clocking in at eight minutes and twenty-eight seconds.

    a) The Beatles' "Hey Jude"
    b) Johnny Cash's "A Boy Named Sue"
    c) Don McLean's "American Pie"
    d) Queen's "Bohemian Rhapsody"

8. In Japanese, number ___ is slang for your "best karaoke song."

    a) 1
    b) 18
    c) 99
    d) 7

9. Which "Power of Love" pop icon costarred as Gwyneth Paltrow's washed-up dad in _Duets_?

    a) Peter Cetera
    b) Kenny Loggins
    c) Huey Lewis
    d) Randy Newman

---

1. a) Opened in 1981, Dimples of Burbank, California, claims to be the first karaoke bar in North America. A famous local joint frequented by celebs, Dimples is known for its rock star-quality talent. **2. c)** Finns have the most karaoke usage per person in the word. Finland is also the home of the **Karaoke World Championships**, an annual competition of karaoke, amateur best. **3. d)** A **KJ** is a karaoke jockey, a DJ for karaoke. **4. b)** Not to be confused with the scene where the in-laws' family broke out into spontaneous performance of "I Say a Little Prayer"), Cameron Diaz won the crowd over with her so-bad-it's-charming performance of "I Just Don't Know What to Do With Myself," Julia Roberts was not going to get the guy. **5. d)** Jay Leno has made public statements against karaoke. Pro-karaoke celebs include Tom Cruise, who has karaoked with Japan's Prime Minister; Rachael Ray, who talks about karaoke on her show; and Amy Tan, who used to sing in a band with Stephen King and Matt Groening. Any band with King and Groening should be considered fake music, a.k.a. karaoke. **6. True.** In 2003, the Sex Pistols mastermind wrote a manifesto about the recycling of British media culture, entitled "Karaoke Culture." It had nothing to do with actual karaoke, and more to do with emergent punk in electronic music. Which leads us to believe McLaren has probably never karaoked before. **7. c)** While each song is ridiculously long and should never be karaoked, Don McLean's "American Pie" is the worst at 8:28. Next up is "Hey Jude" (7:08), the four-part "Bohemian Rhapsody" (5:55), and finally "A Boy Named Sue" (3:44). **8. b)** _Juhachiban_, or number 18, is Japanese slang for "the song you are best at singing." "Eighteen" refers to the eighteen most popular Kabuki plays. **9. c)** Huey Lewis and Gwyneth Paltrow sing "Cruisin'" together at the end of the only mainstream American feature film about karaokers.

ACKNOWLEDGMENTS

Thank you to everyone who has ever stayed with me for just one more song: John "Come Sail Away" Pham, Julie "Jazz Hands" Kim, Leilani "Pirates of Penzance" Trujillo, Parisa "Self-Control" Karami, Sharon "Depeche Mode" Dang, Phillip "Phantom" Tiongson, Aram "Richard Marx" Moshayedi, David "The Gambler" Harlan, Emily "Desperado" Corkill, Paige "Sweet Caroline" Nobles, Derek "I Never Promised You a Rose Garden" Kim, Jason "John Denver" Shiga, Paul "Tainted Love" Choe, Scott Louie, Wilson Ling, Cristina Yoon, Ben "Reminiscing" Andres, Erin "Bette Davis Eyes" Lee, Caroline "I don't karaoke" Hwang, Richard "Alison" Hahn, Faye "Real Love" Ryu, Christina "Genie in a Bottle" Alba, Tina Chiang, Robyn Chapman, Kinping "Complicated" Koo, Christine Niho, Yunny Yip, and the Minibosses for singing with me and Acorn. Also, my cousins Lijay "Irreplaceable" Shih, Leway "Shania Twain" Shih, Jeff "Usher" Hou, Patty "Death Cab" Hou, Aristotle "Pearl Panda" Sun, Argus Sun, and the rest of my loud, singing family.

Special thanks goes to my fabulous agent, Lilly Ghahremani, who still owes me a Journey song. Great appreciation goes to my editor at Chronicle, Kate Prouty, for keeping me in tune.

A super thank you to my contributors: Elisa "Yellow" Paik, Grandpa Shig, Nick "I Hate Myself for Loving You" Austin, Ben "Take On Me" Kim, and David "My Pony, Ride It" Chong for your impeccable music tastes, Sean Lee and Suzette Lee for your unbeatable family photos, Mirra Fine for your fever-inducing dance moves, Natalie Bovis-Nelson, Joni Wilson, the Karaoke Scene message boarders, Heidi Mattila of the Karaoke World Championships, Samantha Sayegh, the folks at Sound Choice, and Flo Apeles for your karaoke-loving spirit.